BEYOND RENEWAL

BEYOND RENEWAL

The Kingdom of God

Brian Hathaway

WORD PUBLISHING

WORD (UK) Ltd
Milton Keynes, England

WORD AUSTRALIA
Kilsyth, Victoria, Australia

STRUIK CHRISTIAN BOOKS (PTY) LTD
Maitland, South Africa

ALBY COMMERCIAL ENTERPRISES PTE LTD
Balmoral Road, Singapore

CHRISTIAN MARKETING NEW ZEALAND LTD
Havelock North, New Zealand

JENSCO LTD
Hong Kong

SALVATION BOOK CENTRE
Malaysia

BEYOND RENEWAL
Copyright © Brian Hathaway 1990

First published by WORD (U.K.) LTD 1990

ISBN 0-85009-339-2 (Australia ISBN 1-86258-091-X)

Unless otherwise noted, all Scripture quotations are either from the New International Version © 1978 International Bible Society, or the author's own translation.

The material contained within the KINGDOM MANIFESTO is not subject to the copyright contained within this book and can be freely copied.

Typesetting by Laser Graphics, Milton Keynes.
Reproduced, printed and bound in Great Britain for WORD (U.K.) LTD by Richard Clay Ltd., Bungay.

CONTENTS

BEYOND RENEWAL

Foreword

This book from a small country in the South Pacific has an urgent message for the Church all around the world. If we do what it urges, the Church will be profoundly transformed.

Some people in the Church have focused on evangelism. Others have majored on social concern. Still others have stressed the gifts and power of the Holy Spirit. Increasingly, theologians and biblical scholars have been urging us to recover the central biblical theme of the Kingdom of God. Brian Hathaway's important book does all these things at once – in a popular readable form that the average lay person can understand.

I first met Brian in 1986 when I visited his wonderful congregation, Te Atatu Bible Chapel in Auckland, New Zealand. I saw an interracial body of believers with native Maoris actively involved with folk of European ancestry. I rejoiced as I learned of numerous social ministries providing jobs and housing people. I was amazed at the rapid church growth (from 90 to 650 in 10 years) and the stories of dramatic conversion of many kinds of folk, even drug addicts. I experienced the powerful pervasive presence of the Holy Spirit in a moving charismatic worship service.

I know that God hears their prayers! When I visited Te Atatu, my home congregation, an inner-city interracial body in Philadelphia, was under heavy pressure from some who objected to our Christ-centred programmes in our community centre. I asked Te Atatu to pray us through and they did.

Beyond Renewal has a balanced, biblical approach that bridges the tragic divisions in the Church today. It is both evangelical and charismatic, both evangelistic and social concerned. All of this is grounded in an over-arching Kingdom theology.

I am more certain today than ever that this is the integrated biblical vision and practice that the Church everywhere desperately needs. The wholistic model that **Beyond Renewal** shares and the integrating theological framework that it presents will, if implemented, lead to one of the most explosive decades of church growth and costly discipleship in Christian history.

Ronald J. Sider, Professor of Theology and Culture, Eastern Baptist Theological Seminary.

Introduction

It was the August vacation, the year was 1969 and I sat at my study desk with a great hunger in my heart.

I had known the Lord for some years. In fact, I could well remember the day in 1953 I had invited Jesus Christ into my life. It was while we were on our family Christmas holiday and after hearing my father preach the gospel in a small church just outside of Nelson.

The year was easy to remember. It was the year of Her Majesty Queen Elizabeth II's first visit to this country and we had all been given little flags to wave. We even stuck them to the outside of our car windows with black rubber suction cups. It was the year of a tragic disaster when over 150 New Zealanders lost their lives after the North-bound Christmas express train plunged into the swollen river near to the sawmilling town of Tangiwai. It was also the year that Edmund Hillary, a New Zealander, and Sherpa Tensing, became the first men to scale Mt Everest.

But these events were far from my mind as I pored over the first eight chapters of the book of Romans during ten intensive days of seeking God.

I had been an active Christian for the sixteen years since my conversion. As a teenager I had gone regularly to our Open Brethren church in a small town about 160 Km north of Wellington, the capital city of New Zealand. I had studied the Bible, taught Sunday School and even witnessed for Christ to my friends at Secondary school and that was a really big issue in those days.   University study took me to Auckland, where I completed a degree in Science, married and then taught in a large Auckland High School.

All of these experiences in life gave me further opportunities to prove my Christian life and serve my Lord. I preached at services, camps, conventions and on street corners. I led several people to Christ, ran childrens' programmes and youth groups. My wife and I even spent some months overseas in missionary work. For young people brought up within the Brethren denomination, missionary work was the pinnacle of Christian service.

As I sat there in my study during that August vacation, I was an elder of a small Open Brethren assembly in West Auckland and actively involved in a variety of successful church activities.

Why did I feel so empty? Why was it that in the midst of a busy Christian life there was a deep longing for more reality and evidence of God in my life?

During university days, in the early 1960's, I met people who claimed to have had an experience with the Holy Spirit and some also spoke in tongues. I was deeply suspicious of these people. We had been taught that Pentecostalism was an off-beat form of Christianity, something more akin to Mormons and Jehovah Witnesses. Yet most of these people were very different to many of the Christians I knew. They loved to talk about Jesus, enjoyed praying and read the Bible enthusiastically. In fact, they were somewhat embarrassing to be around – always praising the Lord and wanting to tell people how great Jesus was. They tended to show up the shallowness of much of my own faith.

As a university student, it was necessary to get employment over the Christmas vacation to pay my way. I found employment in the freezing works. My job was to put up hooks for 10 hours a day, 6 days a week. Not the most stimulating of jobs but the pay was good. While working here I met one of those Pentecostals, Dave by name, who was a young man of my own age. During our lunch times we sat and debated many issues relating to the work of the Holy Spirit.

I can vividly remember Dave showing me his back one morning at our tea break. He had been out in the sun and his back was bright red, very blistered and clearly painful. On meeting at lunch time he again showed me his back. To my utter amazement, it was completely healed. The red colour had disappeared, the blisters were gone and, if I had not seen it earlier in the day, I would not have believed it to be the same back. I immediately assumed that he had had some treatment for it and had gone to the resident nurse. He assured me that he had not. In fact, all he had done was pray that morning that God would heal it. We discussed healing that lunch time and I discovered that my dispensational arguments, (that God didn't do such things in this day and age), were no match for his healed back!! God had my attention!

Over the next few years I read widely about the ministry of the Holy Spirit, attended conferences and listened to tapes. Several times I plucked up enough courage to get people to pray for me, that I might receive a deeper work of the Holy Spirit, yet nothing seemed to change. As I wasn't particularly keen to speak in tongues, I was always tentative and tense during these times of prayer.

By August 1969 I had decided that no matter what it took, I wanted to discover for myself a greater reality in God. My perception of Christianity for most of my life had been that it was largely a set of conditions or rules – 'dos and don'ts', with 'don'ts' seeming to number more than 'dos'. I was now realising that for all the excellent teaching I had received, and all the understanding of God's truth and ways, my form of Christian life had been one of living 'under law'. As I read the first eight chapters of Romans over and over again during that vacation I found that they contained a key word which was to unlock this part of Scripture for me, that word was the word 'law'. It occurs 60 times in these chapters. It was Romans 8:4 which finally lifted the scales from my eyes. 'We are able to meet the Law's requirements, so long as we are living no longer by the dictates of our sinful nature, but in obedience to the promptings of the Spirit' (Phillips translation). I suddenly saw the implications of this statement – all of God's requirements are fulfilled in my life if I live according to the Spirit. It was not a matter of keeping or not keeping rules and regulations, it was a matter of walking and living in the Spirit.

Something happened as that truth penetrated my spirit. It was probably a more radical event in my life than my conversion had been all those years earlier. For the first time I felt free. I now set myself to walk in the Spirit.

After this event my teaching of God's word changed. I sensed a freshness and empowering that I had never known before. Inevitably I started to teach the first eight chapters of Romans. As I taught these chapters, others discovered a new reality in their Christian faith and several people came to faith in Christ. Each day was a new opportunity to test (a good thing for a scientist to do) 'walking in the Spirit'. Around this time, a parent came to see me during a parents' evening at the High school where I was teaching. As I sat there talking to the parent I realised, for the first time, that the Holy Spirit was giving me an insight (a word of knowledge?) about a situation in that family. As I tentatively spoke this out to the lady sitting in front of me, she broke down and wept and I was able to pray with her before she left my office.

From that time to this I have been on a learning curve, seeking to walk more effectively in the Holy Spirit. Opportunities to witness demonic forces fleeing at the name of Jesus, occasional healings, strong convictions from the Holy Spirit to act in certain ways, insight and wisdom into difficult situations, exciting visionary insights, opposition and hostility, and above all, a freshness and authority in teaching the Word of God, have all flowed from that work of God in my life during the days of that vacation. Tongues came much later and have been a further source of encouragement and strength.

The rest of this book is the story of a very ordinary group of Christians living in West Auckland, New Zealand. It covers some of the events and experiences that have affected their lives over the last fifteen years or so.

In fact it is the story of an Open Brethren church which has attempted to adjust to Charismatic Renewal and to institute change. It is a story of struggles and encouragements, learning experiences and mistakes. It is the story of imperfect people working within imperfect structures struggling with incomplete understandings. Of a group of people who deeply appreciated the strengths of their Brethren heritage but recognised that this heritage also had its limitations and weaknesses.

In telling this story some may feel that I have been too hard on our own denomination. If that is so, I apologise in advance. That has not been my intention. I have been the recipient of a fine tradition. My own parents were godly people who brought me up in the knowledge of the Lord and were excellent examples of active, caring and sincere Christians. I could not have wanted for a finer start to life and for this I often thank God. The three Brethren assemblies in New Zealand that I personally have been associated with have all contributed to my spiritual growth in profound ways. I count as some of my best friends people with whom I have fellowshipped in assemblies. We appreciate our heritage, but have a deep sense of sadness over the present state of much of the Brethren movement both in this country and overseas.

Nor is this story an attack on any individuals. I respect those who have been leaders in our Brethren movement over the past 30 years. I have been challenged by their commitment and many times blessed by their ministry.

We tell this story, not to glorify a congregation or any people in this congregation. Rather, it is an attempt to seek to encourage those who desire a deeper work of the Holy Spirit in their personal lives and churches. Churches that seem locked into stagnation and decline need not be afraid of renewal, but should be prepared to embrace the helpful aspects of this movement and work them out within a church framework. Also that those congregations who have experienced renewal and are now perhaps suffering from ingrownness and lack of direction may be able to clarify and outwork the issues which the Holy Spirit seems to be bringing to many churches both in this country and around the world. Things can be changed. God answers prayer and is gracious and faithful to His people. Fresh breath can ignite dull people and sweep through barren places creating growth and bringing blessing. New vision is essential. There's a community to touch and a world to reach for Christ. Old bones can live!

This book is also an attempt to point out to charismatic churches that the results of renewal should go beyond the four walls of the church and out into the local communities. The central theme of Jesus' ministry was the Kingdom of God. A recovery and practical outworking of this is not a current fad but a rediscovery of the heart of the gospel.

During the past 20 or so years many books have been written about how renewal has affected congregations around the world. In what way is this one different? To our knowledge it is the first recounting of how renewal has impacted an Open Brethren assembly.

When compared with mainline denominations, Open Brethren assemblies represent a very small part of the Christian Church. However, this part has had an influence throughout the conservative evangelical world far in excess of its numerical strength. It has produced many hundreds of missionaries who have gone to the farthest parts of this planet, numerous Biblical scholars and many people who have participated whole heartedly in para church organisations around the globe. However, Open Brethren assemblies have by and large been the most resistant to many of the changes which have encompassed much of the Christian world during this time. For this reason we believe that this story should be told.

Unfortunately by reading this book one may probably gain a too glamorous view of our congregation. Te Atatu Bible Chapel does not have it all together. We experience the same pressures and conflicts that most congregations are subject to in a Western materialistic society. Marriages are under pressure, there are struggles in relationships, we face a lack in people's commitment and shortage of finances (this is one area in which there always seem to be more needs than resources to meet them!!).

As a congregation we have commenced a journey. We are travelling along a pathway. We are on a pilgrimage. Our aim is to have a strong supportive congregational base and from here to be more effective within our community. We need to discover and use all the resources that God has provided for us.

We do not presume upon the grace of God. Many churches in New Zealand that have known God's blessing and rapid growth have seen this to be short lived. Our situation may be very different in five years time. We share this simply to give some insights that we have discovered into problems which are common to many congregations of God's people around the world.

It is our prayer that as you read this book you will be encouraged to love the Lord more and seek His Kingdom more earnestly.

PART I

RENEWAL

CHAPTER
ONE

RENEWAL

Tension

The scene is a small church in the Western suburbs of Auckland. It is Sunday evening, mid summer, 1972 and charismatic renewal has been impacting the churches for several years. About 150 people have come together to be led in an evening of worship by two well known Christian song writers and worship leaders, David and Dale Garratt.

During the evening the visiting worship leaders encourage the congregation to raise their hands as part of their worship. Some people do, others don't. Despite the enthusiastic worship and singing, you can sense a degree of tension in the atmosphere.

Next day my telephone runs hot. Several who were at the service on the previous night are objecting strenuously to the hand raising.

'This leads to uncontrollable emotionalism!'

'Next you'll have us all rolling on the floor!'

'What about the weaker brother?'

'Raising hands is inappropriate in church during summer because of the underarm body odour problem,' and so on went the complaints.

Dutifully the eldership met and discussed this delicate matter. Should we permit hand raising in church or should we forbid it? Are there any Biblical guidelines? Where will this lead us? The deliberation ranges over many issues and occupies a considerable amount of time.

Finally it is decided to forbid the raising of hands in public and a suitable statement is made on the next Sunday to the congregation.

Again the telephone runs hot on Monday morning. This

time it is a different group of people but the same degree of agitation.

'Why can't those who wish to raise hands be allowed to?'
'Nobody is saying everybody should raise hands.'
'And anyway who is the weaker brother? Shouldn't we be doing something about his weakness rather than letting him hold us all to ransom?'
'What about 1 Timothy 2:8 – "lifting up holy hands"?' (This latter point is particularly telling because our denomination claimed that we obeyed the Scripture.)

Again the eldership meets. Again much discussion and argument into the late hours of the night. We modify our previous decision to permit the raising of hands but it is only to be half-mast!! Hands will not be raised above the lobe of the right ear and must be held toward the front!!

That should suit everybody. After all it will be very hard to lose emotional control with half-mast hands. It should overcome the underarm body odour problem and the weaker brother mightn't even notice.

Funny now but deadly serious then!!

Charismatic Renewal

Our congregation had been born in 1965 as an off-shoot from a church that had commenced youth work in a nearby suburb. In the early days, there had been tensions over charismatic renewal in the fellowship as a few members had embraced these teachings. Some had been asked to leave and people had been hurt.

Charismatic renewal in the 1960's and 1970's was to have an enormous impact on the churches in our country. An impact which would leave the whole movement severely weakened. It would force thousands of the keenest and most energetic members out into other churches. Some would become leaders of independent congregations, while others would finish up joining or pastoring Baptist churches around the country. Churches would be split, family relationships would be strained and a whole generation of young people would be brought up to be suspicious and fearful of certain aspects of the ministry of the Holy Spirit.

As a congregation we experienced the strains and

difficulties that many churches faced during this period. We saw the changed lives of some in our congregation as they returned from hearing the overseas speakers who were travelling through the country telling of the power of the Spirit and the importance of spiritual gifts.

Tapes and books circulated among members of the congregation. We felt the prickly relationships between various groups in the fellowship – 'the haves' and 'the have nots'. Love was sometimes lacking in the exchanges between people in the specially called meetings to discuss these issues.

At leadership we were divided over these questions. To keep the peace we would sweep the problems under the mat during our meetings. To maintain balance in our preaching we would make sure that a non-charismatic speaker followed a charismatic one. We saw people leave the fellowship. Some because we were going too fast in these areas and others because we were moving too slowly.

To be sure, not everything came up as sweet smelling roses in the charismatic garden. But then life always brings its fair share of problems and young life its immaturity. Some of us remember going to a 'Jesus Crusade' around this time to hear an overseas speaker who had a healing ministry. After the service we were shocked to see a man who had been prayed for with lung cancer and told he was healed, coughing up blood and collapsing in the car park.

We were perplexed about the uniformity of many charismatic services about this time. It was claimed that the Spirit was free to move in such services but a certain predictability, with the mandatory 'singing in the Spirit,' seemed the order of the day. Undoubtedly there was life and excitement. The music was fresh and the singing joyous and worshipful – a far cry from the formality of many church services.

Could charismatic renewal be contained within our type of congregation? Were there Biblical guidelines we could follow to avoid the excesses which we sometimes witnessed around us? Where could we go to learn these? We had no role models in our denomination of congregations which had successfully incorporated this renewal within their framework. At least the Anglicans had St Pauls in Symonds

St and the Baptists had Spreydon in Christchurch. These two churches had broken the ice for renewal in their respective denominations and were the stimulus to renewal impacting many churches throughout the country and spreading rapidly throughout these denominations. This rapid spread was no doubt facilitated by the Baptists annual conference and the Anglican synod. Such a structure with its combined gatherings was not present in our denomination and most congregations were linked to others only by speakers who travelled the country. All of these were opposed to the renewal and most were actively resisting it. Any who showed some interest were hounded out of the movement.

Unity

For six long years after that summer evening in 1972, we vacillated. We watched churches around us mushroom as they embraced charismatic renewal, while we stagnated – immobilised, dispirited and frustrated.

Finally the eldership decided to resolve the charismatic issue. At the commencement of 1978 it was decided that we should set aside one night a month for deliberation.

Many hours were spent in discussions, study of Scripture and the preparation of a paper which was finally presented to the congregation in October of 1978. By the end of this time the elders had come to unity over two main issues. First, we believed that all the gifts of the Spirit should be functioning in churches today. Second, that each Christian needed to know the empowering work of the Holy Spirit. What such a work of the Spirit was termed did not seem to us to be the issue. The real issue – did Christians know in experience, how to walk in the power and life of the Holy Spirit?

We had not completely resolved how these areas would be handled. Neither did we have all answers about many of the practical outworkings of these issues but the leadership was in unity. As a congregation we had commenced a journey. A journey that has continued to this day.

Blessing

At the commencement of 1979 we knew something was different! During the month of January we saw six people come to faith in Christ. January in the Southern Hemisphere is the off-month for church activities. It is mid-summer and New Zealanders are at the many beaches and beautiful holiday areas for which our country is famous. For many of us, we thought that God was on holiday during this month too! Well, if not on holiday, then busy in the Northern hemisphere! Yet here we saw six brand new Christians in one month – more than we'd ever had in one month and it was January. Amazing! Throughout that year and for the next ten years we were to see many hundreds of people come to faith in Christ. In fact, the congregation grew from 90 adults and teenagers (it had been at this level for the 6 previous years) at the commencement of 1979 to about 650 ten years later. Many of those coming to faith in Christ were influenced by friends or family members who were becoming Christians, rather than by evangelistic programmes which we were running. Such growth and congregational size may not seem significant when compared to megachurches overseas but within our country and among congregations of our denomination it was considerable.

Clearly something very important had happened within the church. We put this down to the fact that the leadership had decided to let God's Spirit do whatever He wanted to with no 'ifs', 'buts' or restrictions. Nothing else had changed.

Over the next ten years we were to see people released from demonic power, freed from past crippling experiences, whole families converted and people healed from physical complaints.

CHAPTER TWO

THE MINISTRY OF THE SPIRIT

We were sitting around a kitchen table discussing the ministry of the Holy Spirit. It was late and the arguments had ranged far and wide that night. Bruce, Graham and I had been in our denomination for all of our Christian lives and during our younger days there seemed to have been an embargo on any teaching on the Holy Spirit. I was well into my twenties before I heard any public teaching from teachers in our denomination on the necessity to be filled with the Spirit of God, even though I had attended Christmas and Easter conventions throughout our country for most of my life. Speakers at that time appeared to be afraid to teach on this topic. However more recently there had been much more discussion about the Spirit's ministry. It was the mid 1970's and many people were leaving our congregations to become involved in the renewal which had touched most mainline denominations.

The arguments of that evening were familiar.

Prophecy did away with Scripture!

Pentecostals were away with the fairies!

Healings were faked and healing meetings were nothing but mass hysteria! Anyway, if the gift of healing was operating today why didn't people with that gift go into the hospitals and heal all the sick?

Tongues were of the devil! It had been proved that this was the case – a person had spoken in tongues in a southern town and a Maori brother said he was blaspheming in Maori!

How could a person have any more of the Holy Spirit than they'd received at conversion?

Sign gifts had ceased, 1 Corinthians 13:8 said so!

Charismatics put themselves on a pedestal! Those who spoke in tongues got into immorality! And so on went the objections.

We didn't make much progress that night and I went away with a sad heart. Sad at the apparent blindness which intolerant opposition to the current move of the Holy Spirit so often seemed to bring. I had unfortunately seen this many times before in people brought up in our congregations. We could talk about most other things but when the topic of the Holy Spirit was raised a barrier came down, the atmosphere would become tense, people would fidget and eyes would glaze over.

At that time our own congregation was divided over the issue of the work of the Holy Spirit and that is why I had gone to see these two men who were in our fellowship. They had been upset about some of the speakers we had been having and the direction that they perceived the fellowship was moving in.

Some months later Bruce was to pick up the local newspaper and see an advertisement for a week-long marriage seminar conducted by an American speaker. Unknown to Bruce, and his wife Lilian, this man was a Pentecostal but they went along and greatly appreciated his teaching. That is until Sunday morning when he gave his testimony and explained how he was touched by the Holy Spirit, spoke in tongues and moved in some of the gifts of the Spirit.

Bruce was very confused when Lilian went forward to be filled with the Spirit after that service. In fact, he was confused for some days! However he could not argue with the change he saw in his wife. He searched the Scriptures. He spent sleepless nights tossing and turning and wrestling with issues. He had difficulty eating. How could God do this to him and upset all his theology?

Finally he gave in and told God that he too wanted all that His Spirit had for him. He made a promise to the Holy Spirit that he would always seek to do whatever He directed him to do. His life was turned upside-down! God blessed his business – he saw numerous staff and clients come to the Lord during the next year. New ministries opened up to him and his wife. The first time he gave his testimony in public the Holy Spirit gave him an insight into the life of a person in the audience which deeply affected this person's life. Since that time the

Spirit of God has blessed their ministry together and touched many lives through them.

Were Bruce and Lilian Christians before this event? Yes. Did they love the Lord? Yes. Were they seeking to serve Him faithfully? Yes – they were teaching in the Sunday School. Did they read the Word? Yes. Were they born again by the Holy Spirit? Yes.

Well, what had happened? They had been filled, blessed, empowered, released, baptised, drenched, touched, anointed, renewed in the Spirit! No point in arguing over which word to use when the results of such a deep work of the Spirit were so obvious.

In the years since that time we have seen many people come into a deeper work of the Holy Spirit. Some have come from very conservative church backgrounds and have loved the Lord for most of their lives. Others have been relatively new Christians. Many young people have been touched by God and these include children of those of us in the eldership. Not all have had such a radical turn around as Bruce and Lilian. For some it has been a quiet, growing and deeper appreciation of various aspects of the Spirit's ministry. Others have moved into the experience of new gifts, to the blessing of the whole congregation.

The Spirit in Jesus

Amidst all the controversy, strife over terminology and confusion regarding the ministry of the Holy Spirit which has swirled around churches over the past 25 years, we have discovered one irrefutable fact – Christ performed His ministry here on earth through the power and work of the Holy Spirit. For those of us brought up in conservative evangelical churches where Christ had been so central in our teaching, discovering this point has helped us work through the issues. Tucked away in the New Testament are some very significant statements about the Holy Spirit's ministry in the life of Jesus. Studying these confronts us with a whole new understanding of the Spirit's work.

For many years I believed that Jesus was somehow more than human in the way He lived. After all, He was God on earth and thus had a distinct advantage over us mere mortals.

However, I have discovered that the New Testament seems to indicate that Jesus made use of the same resources that we do to live His life on earth. Which means, in fact, that He was truly human. Maybe in the past I emphasised the deity of Christ at the expense of His humanity and therefore missed some very vital and practical understandings which would have helped me to live my Christian life more effectively.

We read in Luke 2:5 'Jesus grew in wisdom and stature, and in favour with God and men.' Thus He grew intellectually (in wisdom), physically (in stature), spiritually (in favour with God), and socially (in favour with men). Scripture also tells us that He learned obedience by the things that He suffered (Hebrews 5:6) and that He was also tempted in all points as we are (Heb 4:15).

As a Jewish lad He would have been educated in the synagogue, developing His mental abilities. He ate, slept, walked from place to place and learned a trade, thus functioning in a normal physical manner just as we do.

No doubt He developed relationships with people – His family, friends, neighbours and others in society. Thus He matured socially in a similar way as we do.

Is it not reasonable to suggest that He also matured spiritually in just the same way as we do? We read in Philippians 2:6-8 that Jesus 'made Himself nothing', 'became a servant', 'was made in human likeness' and 'humbled himself.' What in fact He was doing was restricting himself as the Son of God to live within the limitations of the same resources which are available to us, His followers.

Clearly He was a true and complete human being.

Spiritual resources

There are at least four basic resources for spiritual growth: prayer, scripture, faith (linked to obedience) and the ministry of the Holy Spirit. Jesus made use of them all.

There is no doubt about the participation of Jesus in the first two. He was often praying, and had a deep understanding of the purposes of God as revealed in the Old Testament writings.

Faith simply means trusting and obeying God, and Jesus spoke many times of the intimacy of this relationship with the

Father and His commitment and obedience to the will of the Father. A study of these aspects of the life of Jesus is very rewarding in itself but it is to the ministry of the Holy Spirit in His life which we will now turn.

Old Testament prophecies

Three very clear prophecies in the book of Isaiah predicted that the Spirit of God would be on Jesus. In Isaiah 11:2 we read, 'The Spirit of the Lord will rest upon him – the Spirit of wisdom and of understanding . . . counsel . . . power . . . knowledge and of the fear of the Lord.' Isaiah 42:1 says,'Here is my servant . . . I will put my Spirit on him and He will bring justice to the nations.' Isaiah 61:1 is particularly well known, 'The Spirit of the Sovereign Lord is upon me, because the Lord has anointed me to preach good news to the poor. He has sent me to bind up the brokenhearted, to proclaim freedom to the captives and release from darkness for the prisoners.' The significance of these prophecies about the coming Messiah has often been noted. When the fulfilment of two of these prophecies regarding the ministry of the Holy Spirit in the life of Christ are drawn attention to in the New Testament as well (Is 42:1, Is 61:1) this should alert us to the importance of this topic.

Conception

In Luke 1:35 the angel says to Mary, 'The Holy Spirit will come upon you, and the power of the Most High will overshadow you. So the holy one to be born of you will be called the Son of God.' (NIV) Jesus was conceived by the power of the Holy Spirit. The commencement of His life on earth was accomplished by the work of the Spirit. At that mysterious moment the power of the most High overshadowed Mary and our Lord's life on earth commenced.

For the Christian we see a parallel here. We commence our Christian journey by being born into the Kingdom of God through the work of the Spirit. In John 3:5 we read, 'No one can enter the Kingdom of God unless he is born of water and the Spirit.'

The Spirit came upon Him

At the baptism of Jesus we learn that the Holy Spirit came on Him as the voice of the Father was heard confirming Him to be His Son. (Luke 3:22). This was a very significant event for Jesus, marking the commencement of His public ministry. In a similar way His disciples were told not to leave Jerusalem to commence their public ministry until the Holy Spirit came on them.

Unfortunately so many well-meaning Christians are involved in serving God and have no practical knowledge of the ministry of the Spirit. They have never known this anointing and equipping ministry of the Holy Spirit. Billy Graham is reputed to have asked the question as to how much Christian activity would carry on completely unaffected if God removed His Spirit from the earth. How much of my own ministry would continue on unaffected? For Jesus to do the will of the Father without knowing the ministry of the Spirit seems to have been an impossibility.

Full of the Holy Spirit

After His baptism, Luke records that Jesus was full of the Holy Spirit (Luke 4:1). Such an event is also recorded of others in the New Testament. The filling of the Holy Spirit in both the Old and New Testaments seems to have been a clearly recognisable occasion, one which onlookers noticed either at the time of the initial event or subsequently in its effects in the lives of the people.

Just as Jesus needed to be filled with the Holy Spirit, so the Christian is commanded to be constantly filled with the Spirit (Ephesians 5:18).

Led by the Spirit

Returning from the Jordan, Jesus is led by the Spirit into the wilderness to be tempted by the devil (Luke 4:1). For the Son of God to need to be led by the Holy Spirit is remarkable enough in itself, but to be led into the wilderness to be tempted by the devil is almost beyond our understanding.

Galatians 5:18 indicates that it should be the normal experience of Christians to be led by the Holy Spirit.

Power of the Spirit

After His temptation Jesus is said to have returned to Galilee in the power of the Spirit (Luke 4:14). It could have been assumed that being the Son of God, Jesus would have had power *(dunamis)* of His own. However it seems that He, like us, was dependent on the Holy Spirit for this empowering.

What's more, Jesus enters the synagogue and reads Isaiah 61, telling all those who heard Him that this prophecy, about the ministry of the Spirit in His life, was being fulfilled at that moment in time. In addition, the prophecy told them that this anointing of the Holy Spirit enabled Jesus to fulfil the ministry that His Father had called Him to do.

Spoke in the power of the Spirit

John's gospel tells us that Jesus spoke the words of God because God had given Him the Spirit without limit (John 4:34). The sermon on the Mount, the parables, the words of counsel and encouragement, the wise answers to scheming questions, all these and more were inspired and empowered by the Holy Spirit.

Matthew records the fulfilment of the prophecy of Isaiah 42 where he reminds his readers that the Holy Spirit was on Jesus to enable Him to 'proclaim justice to the nations'. (Matthew 12:18)

Most significantly, in those last strategic days just before leaving this earth, Luke records very specifically that Jesus instructed His disciples through the Holy Spirit (Acts 1:2).

The same resources and power of the Holy Spirit are available for the Christian in areas of speaking and teaching. Specific gifts of the Holy Spirit are bestowed on His people for this purpose.

Authority over spiritual powers

When Jesus was accused of casting out demons by the power of Satan, He calmly refuted this accusation. He said that it was by the Spirit of God that He cast out demons and this demonstrated that the Kingdom of God had come among them (Matthew 12:25;28). Again we see the Son of God drawing on the resources of the Spirit as He drove back the forces of Satan to establish the Kingdom of God.

For the Christian there is a clear message here – as the Kingdom of God was established on earth through the power of the Spirit in the life of Christ, so it is for His followers.

Healing and doing good

Peter tells his Gentile listeners in the home of Cornelius that God anointed Jesus with the Holy Spirit and as a result He went about doing good and healing all who were under the power of the devil (Acts 10:38). Thus we see that the healing ministry of Jesus was achieved through the ministry of the Holy Spirit in His life – as were the many other good things that He did.

Today the gift of healing is also sometimes bestowed by the Holy Spirit on the followers of Jesus (1 Corinthians 12:9) and James encourages elders to pray for the sick (James 5:13-16).

Joy by the Spirit

Tucked away in Luke 10:21 is a little statement which is very easy to miss. We read that Jesus was full of joy through the Holy Spirit. Here is a clear evidence that the fruit of the Spirit (joy) was evidenced in the life of Jesus.

We know that this, and other qualities of character are the fruit of the Spirit and are to be seen in the lives of Christians (Galatians 5:22).

Declared to be the Son of God

The Apostle Paul, as he commences his letter to the Christians in Rome, tells his readers that Jesus 'through the Spirit of holiness was declared with power to be the Son of God – Jesus Christ our Lord' (Romans 1:4). Here we see that it was the Holy Spirit who authenticated both the divinity and the Lordship of Christ.

There is a parallel here for the believer in that the Spirit testifies that Christians are God's children (Romans 8:16). The Spirit also authenticates our relationship to God.

Death and Resurrection

As we come to the climax of Christ's ministry on earth we find that this too is achieved through the ministry of the Holy

Spirit. We read that 'Christ through the eternal Spirit offered Himself unblemished to God' (Hebrews 10:14) and that it was the Spirit who raised Jesus from the dead (Romans 8:11). What an amazing thing that the main purpose for Christ's coming to earth, His death and resurrection, were both accomplished by the ministry of the Holy Spirit in His life.

The Christian is encouraged to 'put to death by the Spirit the deeds of the flesh'(Romans 8:13), and reminded that 'the Spirit will give life to our mortal bodies' (Romans 8:11).

Vindicated by the Spirit

Then, just in case we have missed any area of the life of Christ, Paul tells Timothy that the mystery of godliness is great. 'Jesus appeared in a body, and was vindicated by the Spirit' (1 Timothy 3:16). Expressing this another way we could say that while on earth (in the body), and in every possible way, Jesus was shown to be who He really was by the Holy Spirit.

We see that every aspect of Christ's life came under the direction and empowering of the Holy Spirit. His conception, words, authority, miracles, death and resurrection were through the filling, leading and empowering of the Spirit. In fact it seems that there was no significant area in the life of Jesus which was not influenced by the ministry of the Spirit. In a similar way, Christians are to experience this ministry of the Spirit in all areas of their lives.

Obviously we will never fully understand the relationship between the humanity and deity of Christ, and to try to do so leaves us with many unanswered questions. Neither will we ever be able to plumb to its fullest the relationship between the Son and His Father or the Son and the Holy Spirit while here on earth. But scripture clearly shows us that He lived in close relationship with the Father and the Spirit.

If Jesus, the Son of God, needed the equipping and empowering of the Spirit, then how much more do we, His followers and servants? If Christ could not achieve the call of God on His life without the activity of the Spirit, then how can we? Here all arguments about the necessity or otherwise for the ministry of the Spirit in the believer's life must stop.

From day to day and in a personal and practical way, we should set ourselves to humbly and prayerfully seek to experience the work of the Spirit of God in our lives.

CHAPTER
THREE

GIFTS OF THE SPIRIT

Being brought up in our fellowships, with a Scofield Bible and a dispensationalist framework (a belief that God's activity in human history is divided into periods or dispensations), has meant that we had been taught that some of the gifts of the Holy Spirit were not to be expected in this day and age. We never did find out exactly which ones were in and which ones were out!

Clearly the most controversial was the list in 1 Cor 12:8-10. Our Bible teachers could quite easily dismiss tongues, prophecy, healing, miracles, but what about faith? Did George Muller, a great Brethren leader, have a gift of faith? Or what about the gifts of wisdom and knowledge, surely these would be helpful gifts for today? Some of our leaders had seen people experiencing genuine deliverance from the occult. How could you engage in such a ministry without the gift of discerning of spirits? Wasn't this gift listed in the first Corinthians passage? Upon what basis should we include one and eliminate another?

Inevitably, the gifts of tongues, prophecy, healing and miracles seemed to be the most difficult for people from our background to accept and these were the most discussed.

Tongues

One of the strong impressions we received while growing up in our denomination was that those who spoke in tongues were at best a bit simple and at worst demonically controlled. We were told that tongues, as practised today, was some sort of gibberish or baby talk. However many of the people we met who spoke in tongues, impressed us with their maturity. In fact they were often highly intelligent and many had been university trained – most definitely they did not seem to be demonically inspired. Many lived lives of deep devotion to the Lord, loved His Word and shared their faith regularly with people. It saddened us to hear leaders of our movement urging assemblies to 'send such people down the road to the Pentecostals where they belonged.' Many of these people were among the keenest Christians in a fellowship and often the most highly motivated. To send them down the road seemed like we were 'slitting our wrists to save our life!'

Many churches took the position that tongues ceased on the completion of the writing of the New Testament. Evidence for this was said to have been 1 Corinthians 13:10 (when that which is perfect is come). The 'perfect' was defined to be the completion of Scripture and when this occurred, then, these gifts passed away. Such an interpretation was thoroughly bad exegesis but believed by many Brethren people. It is clear from verse 12 that the writer is referring to the return of Christ – 'we shall see face to face'. A quick check of commentaries held in a Christian book shop during the early years of the Charismatic controversy showed that sixteen out of the seventeen commentaries on this portion interpreted the perfect to be the return of Christ. Only one said it referred to the completion of Scripture and this one was written by a person from a strongly dispensationalist background.

With all the negative things we had been brought up to accept about the gift of tongues, it was a surprise to find 14 positive statements in 1 Corinthians 14.

We are encouraged to eagerly desire spiritual gifts (v1) and one of those is tongues. Isn't speaking to God (v2) a good thing? Uttering mysteries (v2) may be strange and beyond the understanding of a scientifically trained mind, but that doesn't mean it has no significance.

Surely building oneself up (v4) has value while edifying the church with tongues and interpretation (v5) Paul says has even more value. Clearly the apostle felt tongues was useful as he wanted everybody to use the gift (v5). Using the gift of tongues means my spirit is praying (v14). The person may not understand what he or she is saying but that doesn't make it a futile exercise. Paul himself was committed to continuing to praying and singing in the spirit (v15). In fact it seems that sometimes when a person is speaking in tongues, thanks is being expressed (v17). Not only that, but God speaks to people through tongues (v21) and it is a sign to unbelievers (v22). The Holy Spirit clearly expects tongues to be used when the congregation is together (v26). The gift can be used up to three times during a congregational service if interpretation is included (v27). If tongues was simply a gift by which the gospel could be preached in a foreign language and there were people of more than three foreign languages present in a church service, then some people would not be able to hear the gospel during a service. Then, as if to clinch the matter once and for all, the apostle says we are not to legislate against the use of the gift of tongues (v39).

We had often heard it argued that tongues was being used in a somewhat selfish manner in the Corinthian Church. That was no doubt true but this does not mean 'tongues' were useless. Even a superficial reading of 1 Corinthians 14 shows that Paul was not recommending non-use, but proper use, a point often missed by our Bible teachers.

Many of us were to discover that tongues, far from being an emotional, uncontrollable outburst, was a valuable gift. It often brought a person closer to the Lord and could be used when a person was not certain how to pray in a particular situation. When combined with interpretation during a service it would bring a deeper sense of the presence of God to those gathered.

Prophecy

If tongues are so useful then according to 1 Corinthians 14 prophecy is much better (v5)!

The first time this gift was used in public in our congregation was by a retired Apostolic minister who had a mature prophetic gifting. After his deep voice had boomed out a 'Thus saith the Lord' there was a stunned silence in the congregation, a bit like what might happen if someone had just spoken some vile profanity in church. When he had finished nobody was quite sure what to do and clusters of saints, in obvious and vigorous discussion, were seen debating its content! In desiring gifts, prophecy is especially to be desired (1 Cor 14:1). The Corinthian church was encouraged to be eager to prophesy (v5). Prophecy strengthens, encourages and comforts (v3) and edifies the whole church (v4). Paul would like all to prophesy (v5) and says all can prophesy in church (v31).

We are left in no doubt that this gift is a more suitable gift than tongues and to be in regular use during congregational services.

One of the problems that conservative Evangelicals face in accepting the validity of the gift of prophecy for today is the belief that prophecy, by its definition, must supersede and add to Scripture.

There is no doubt that the prophetic ministry of Jesus was quite unique and of greater authority than that of Old Testament prophets or John the Baptist. John himself said that there was one coming after him who was greater than he. This was no doubt true about Christ's prophetic ministry as well as the overall effect of His total ministry.

Similarly, is it not reasonable to suggest that the prophetic ministry of the Old Testament prophets (eg Isaiah, Jeremiah), and New Testament (John the Baptist and John the Apostle – book of Revelation), is different to that of the gift of prophecy found in 1 Corinthians 14? Clearly prophecy of 1 Corinthians 14 and that of the prophet in Ephesians 4 are different. All can prophesy in 1 Corinthians 14, while only some are prophets in Ephesians 4. In the New Testament the prophetic word is judged (1 Corinthians 14:29) as to its accuracy. In the Old Testament the prophet was judged (and put to death!) if not accurate (Deut 18:17-22).

Thus, it seems that there are various categories of the prophetic gifting referred to in Scripture and it is certainly not necessary to equate prophecy (1 Corinthians 14) with Old Testament prophets or with the writing of Scripture.

Once this point is understood the use of the gift of prophecy in today's Church becomes much less threatening. In fact, it frees us to enjoy it in the way God meant it to be used – for encouragement, comfort and strengthening (1 Cor 14:3).

Prophetic word does not always have to be predictive. Basically, a 'prophecy' is an inspired message which has limited, if any, previous preparation. A 'teaching' on the other hand is normally an instructional message which has a considerable degree of previous preparation. The origin of both of these is the same, the Holy Spirit. The best prophetic word comes from those who spend much time before the Lord and in His Word, as of course does the best teaching. Some would say that there has been a continual struggle throughout Church history between the teachers and the prophets. Prophecy has visionary and inspirational elements in it, while teaching is normally rational and reasoned; it is dealing with doctrine and tending to be conservative. Prophecy speaks to the heart and conscience, teaching tends to speak to the mind. It is interesting to note that the church at Antioch had both prophets and teachers (Acts 13:1). What balance!

When a genuine gift of prophecy operates we should not elevate what is said to some pinnacle of divine revelation which can not be challenged.

Inspired? Yes!

Infallible? No!

Most certainly what is said must not disagree with Scripture but neither should it be equated with Scripture. The person through whom a prophetic word is brought is not perfect and inevitably colours what is said with his or her own thoughts, expressions and terminology. We are told that 'we prophesy in part' (1 Cor 13:9) which must mean that any prophetic word is not complete – we do not have God's full revelation on this matter. We are also to test prophecy (1 Thess 5:19-21) and prophets are to weigh up what is said by other prophets and to be subject to each other (1 Cor 14:29-32).

One of the simplest ways we have found of testing prophecy is to record it and then transcribe it. Over a period of time we have built up a large file of prophetic messages. In this way we can assess those whom God is obviously gifting in the prophetic ministry. A person who regularly brings accurate and encouraging prophetic words may well be moving towards being recognised as a prophet in the terms of Ephesians 4.

'Don't despise prophesyings'. 'Don't forbid tongues'. The scripture is abundantly clear. Unfortunately we have all too often disobeyed these two specific commands.

Does God speak today?

Observing the world-wide Christian scene over the past 25 years raises the following crucial question – Does God speak to and through human beings today? If the answer to this question is 'No' then prophecy, words of wisdom, words of knowledge, tongues with interpretation are just from the human mind and are no more significant than any other human utterances. On the other hand, if they are, as the Bible says, from the Holy Spirit, (1 Cor 12:4-6) then God is directly involved in this process and we must treat them accordingly. It seems reasonable to believe that God does speak today and in more ways than just through the Scriptures.

Extra-biblical guidance is obviously needed if a missionary is ever to sense God's call to most of the mission fields around the world. We do not read the words Nigeria, Thailand, China, New Guinea or Bolivia in Scripture but many missionaries have served the Lord in these countries during this century. To have been 'called' by God into these countries clearly means that some form of non-scriptural guidance is needed. This is not to doubt that a person's initial call to a mission field can come through reading the Bible, but the geographical location and type of ministry in which a person will be engaged needs to be ascertained in other ways. We must accept that God can and does lead through means other than scripture.

John 10 seems to clearly indicate that Jesus expected His followers to hear His voice. Stated positively, the sheep listen to His voice (v3,16,27). He calls His sheep (v4) and they know His voice (4). Negatively, they do not recognise strangers (v5) and do not listen to thieves and robbers (v8). To limit the positive statements of this portion to the influence of the Scripture alone seems to push these sayings of our Lord to an extreme which I am sure He was not meaning. Clearly, the recognising of a stranger's voice (v5) would be outside of the reference point of scripture. If Satan can tempt why can't the Holy Spirit prompt?

Led by the Spirit

The experience of many in our fellowship over recent years has been that of learning to recognise the promptings of the Holy Spirit in the many and varied ways that He seeks to impress these upon us. Paul urges us to be led by the Spirit (Gal 5:18), to live by the Spirit (Gal 5:25) and to keep in step with the Spirit (Gal 5:25). There seems to be an intuitive work of the Holy Spirit which sometimes bypasses human, rational thought. This is the way that the gifts such as prophecy, word of knowledge and discerning of spirits seem to function.

Romans 8:16 says, 'The Spirit himself bears witness with our spirit that we are God's children.' This is particularly illuminating in regard to the intuitive work of the Holy Spirit. A Christian should know a deep resonating work of the Holy Spirit in the human spirit, confirming our place in God. Over the past 15 years we have observed this ministry of the Spirit in many young Christians. In our experience, the need for assurance of salvation is almost nil for a young Christian brought up in an atmosphere where the ministry of the Spirit is taught and expected. However, for many young people brought up without such an emphasis, assurance of salvation was a recurring problem. Young Christians from such a background often wonder if they are truly Christians and sometimes need constant reassurance. Such assurance is normally encouraged by the reading of verses such as John 1:12 and then being mentally convinced that they had 'received Him' and were therefore 'sons of God'. Some young Christians have been known to recommit their lives to God over and over again just in case the last time didn't work! Those whom we have seen experience this deeper work of the Spirit, seldom doubt their salvation again – 'the Spirit witnesses' this fact. Bring new Christians into the filling, empowering work of the Spirit at conversion and they should never have to doubt or need to be 'intellectually' convinced that they are a child of God.

This does not mean that Scripture is less important than the work of the Holy Spirit in giving a young Christian assurance. Ideally the Word and Spirit should go together. Word without Spirit becomes little more than an intellectual exercise.

Miracles and healing
This topic is a much fought-over aspect of Christian truth

and it is unlikely that anything fresh can be said about it. To come from a position of non-recognition of these gifts to a place of acceptance and subsequent personal experience has been a long struggle for many of us.

There is considerable and growing evidence from around the world that where miracles and healings are being evidenced, the Church is growing very rapidly. The emphasis on signs and wonders over the past few years has increased widely. To dismiss this as irrelevant or some sort of hocus pocus seems to be burying one's head in the sand. It is now estimated that about 20% of the total Christian world embraces areas of charismatic, pentecostal or third wave theology (the percentage is much higher if only the committed Christian world is considered). This portion of the Christian Church employs 25% of the Church's full-time workers and is experiencing 50% of the worldwide Church growth. Much of this evidence of the supernatural is being recorded in the so called 'two thirds world,' but the fact that it is happening at all in this age means we can no longer restrict such a ministry of the Holy Spirit to the first century. The theological debate for conservative evangelicals seems to be shifting from 'whether' the miraculous occurs to 'how' it occurs.

The word 'miracle' as used in 1 Corinthians 12:10 has an air about it which raises considerable alarm in the minds of most conservative Christians. That we can perform miracles, even with the power of the Holy Spirit, is strongly resisted. However where we read the word 'miracles', the Greek phrase used – *energemata dunameon* – could be translated as 'workings of powers' or 'energisings of power'. To be a vehicle for an energising work of God's power does not seem to be nearly as threatening as a performer of a miracle. Jesus also has this phrase used of Him in Mark 6:14 where some people were saying that Jesus was John the Baptist raised from the dead, 'That was why miraculous powers are at work in Him.'

In verse 6 of I Corinthians 12, Paul uses the same Greek word when he says, 'There are different kinds of energisings *(energematon)*, but the same God energises *(energon)* all of them in all people.' Or in verse 11 – 'All of these (gifts) are the energising *(energei)* of one and the same Spirit and he gives them to each one as he determines.' Maybe if the translators had used this terminology rather than miracles, we would have felt more comfortable about this area.

Similar terminology translated as 'working', is used several other times in the New Testament – Ephesians 1:19-20, 'the energising of his mighty strength.' Ephesians 3:7, Paul was 'a servant of this gospel . . . through the energising of his power'. Here, 'energising of his power' could well be translated 'miracle.' Paul was a servant of the gospel through a miracle! Ephesians 3:20, 'He is able to do more than we can ask or think according to his power which energises us'. Colossians 1:29, 'To this end I labour, struggling with all his energy, which so powerfully energises me.' Is it not conceivable, that the Spirit of God, from time to time, gives special ability (energy) to get a task done, or to bring a radical change in a situation, maybe a healing, or some other supernatural event? This certainly seems to have been so in the case of Christ. We read 'people touched him because power was coming from him and healing them all' (Luke 6:19).On another occasion Jesus said 'Someone touched me ; I know power has gone out of me' (Luke 8:46). Or what does it mean when we read, 'The power of the Lord was present to heal'? (Luke 5:17).

For many of us such an explanation is quite foreign to our Western, non-miraculous framework. It borders on the metaphysical and leaves numerous unanswered questions. To understand how such an activity of the Holy Spirit operates, or give adequate scientific explanation is difficult but we must address the Biblical record. Is it possible that we are dealing here with divine energy which can apparently operate through human vessels? This is not to be confused with New Age channelling, which most probably taps into the demonic. Incidentally, isn't it strange that many of us find it easier to accept that Satan can display such power through human beings, than that the Spirit of God can use His power in this way!

Whatever the answer to this question, it's quite clear that such activity is the work of the Holy Spirit (1 Corinthians 12:10,11). The Spirit also gives 'manifestations' *(Gk phanerosis)* of His presence (1 Corinthians 12:7). This word means 'outshinings or appearances' of the Spirit. Such a concept conveys the idea of separate, discrete events, under the control and direction of the Holy Spirit. These can apparently operate in anyone, provided, (presumably) they are indwelt by the Spirit of God.

There is no doubt that this area is open to abuse and many unwise things have occurred in the name of Christ. Such abuse is very unfortunate because it hardens Christian attitudes towards any recognition of the miraculous, and brings a reproach to the name of Christ from the unbelievers.

The Manila Manifesto (Lausanne Congress on Evangelism 1989) states –

'We reject both the skepticism which denies miracles and the presumption which demands them, both the timidity which shrinks from the fullness of the Spirit and the triumphalism which shrinks from the weakness in which Christ's power is made perfect.'

This summarises the position which the leadership of our congregation has taken over the past 10 years. Inevitably we have oscillated between skepticism and presumption during this time. We have many unanswered questions but have seen some evidences of God's miraculous power as we have sought to be open to this dimension.

The 'sign gifts' learning curve

One of the secrets to maintaining unity within a congregation as it moves towards a greater understanding of the I Cor 12 gifts is to recognise that people will be on a continuum of learning.

Believers in our assembly have taken the following spectrum of views on the "sign gifts".(See Figure 1).

a. Believe they ceased at end of first century

Such people normally come from a conservative evangelical background and have had considerable dispensational teaching on this point of view. The view is often held very firmly and people believing it sometimes have quite an emotional reaction to any discussion about this matter.

b. *Not certain as to whether they are valid for today*

Many people have been forced to examine the previous point of view in the light of the impact the charismatic movement has been having in the Christian Church. Obvious changes in the lives of friends or family who have become involved in things of the Spirit have shaken previously held positions.

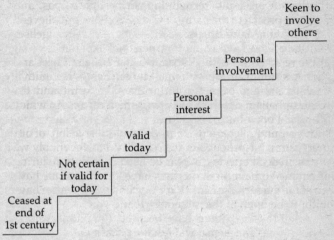

Figure 1. Positions people take on the 'sign gifts'.

c. *'Sign Gifts' are valid for today*

It is a relatively short step from the previous position to this one. There is a cautious, detached, intellectual acceptance that these things are for today. Such a position is often summed up by the following attitude – 'If others seek and experience these gifts then that is OK but I do not want to become personally involved'.

d. *Personal interest and seeking*

Those who come to a position of accepting the 'sign gifts' for today, if they are consistent, will probably gradually move towards a personal and practical interest in this area. This may lead to a prayerful seeking and desiring of spiritual gifts from God (1 Corinthians 12:31, 14:1, 14:39).

e. *Personal participation*

Many in our assembly have come to a personal experience of 'sign gifts'. As these gifts have been used to the edifying of the people themselves (in the case of tongues) or the edifying of others, it has led to growth in many people's lives.

f. *Keen to involve others*

Those who have come to a personal experience of sign gifts are often keen to propagate their beliefs. There is, of course, nothing wrong with this. Human beings are normally keen to share good news with others. Unfortunately they sometimes go about this in an unwise manner and it can cause offence. Very often this creates a 'haves' and 'have nots' situation and allegations of pride may be levelled at those practising and propagating these gifts. However, we have discovered that pride can rear its head in both camps. Pride of having something that others haven't got, but also pride that says 'I haven't got it, I don't want it and I'm quite content with where I am at the moment – thank you'.

All of these positions have been held in our assembly at various times and even now we have a considerable spectrum of views. Recognising that there is such a variety of views and being prepared to accept each other's position must be the first step towards maintaining unity. All of us are on a pilgrimage and many of us have progressively moved through the above stages of personal development with regard to 'sign gifts'.

It is the extremes on the above spectrum of views (points a & f) where most problems occur and most heat is generated. Emotions can run very high in people who hold these views. Intolerance of others may surface. Dogmatic statements are made and inflexible positions adopted. Great sensitivity and pastoral care is required by leaders in supporting and encouraging people when such conflicting positions are held.

Our leadership would not agree on every point regarding 'sign gifts'. In fact they would fit in several of the categories listed above. Since 1978 however, none have taken the position that the 'sign gifts' ceased at the end of the first century.

The following guidelines have been helpful for us as we worked through these controversial issues regarding the ministry of the Holy Spirit.

*   Major on love and acceptance of each other. Seek to structure for close committed relationships, teach on it and model it at leadership.
*   Teach what the scripture has to say on all the gifts. Don't forbid any gifts. The only restrictions that should be placed on gifts of the Spirit are those that the scripture places on them.
*   Encourage people to expect God to 'do more than we can ask or think', and to seek all that God has for them so they can more effectively serve Him.
*   Do not allow pressure to be placed on people by others who have differing viewpoints.
*   Teach people to respond practically to the voice and ministry of the Holy Spirit and to obey Him rather than people.
*   Test all things and hold to what is good (1 Thessalonians 5:21). Encourage people to respond objectively rather than emotionally to controversial issues.
*   Listen to and learn from others across the Body of Christ. Permit interaction, both at leadership and congregational levels with those of differing denominational or theological viewpoints. We have been greatly blessed by input from different streams in the Body of Christ.
*   Be prepared for people to make mistakes as they learn to function in these gifts, especially when using them in public. It seems to be easier to be more tolerant of mistakes that have been made by people preaching, teaching or praying in public than when people prophesy or speak in tongues.
*   Encourage the balance between knowing and doing, theory and practice, doctrine and experience.

Viewing this from our background I believe that congregations from our denomination are better suited to handle a renewing work of the Holy Spirit than many other churches. Their autonomy means that they can embrace changes without reference or control from higher governing bodies. Their multiple leadership preserves them from the extremes and weaknesses of the one person leadership. Their love for and knowledge of God's Word gives a very solid base for Biblical decision making. Their high level of lay involvement means many people can expect to participate in what God wants to do in a congregation. Such features are ideally suited to embracing and preserving a deeper work of God. Unfortunately this has not often been the case and this is sad indeed.

CHAPTER FOUR

CHANGE

General Booth of the Salvation Army once said, 'You can't alter the future without disturbing the present'. Very often churches have earnestly desired changes to occur, could see all the advantages of such changes but leaders have lacked the courage to make the decisions which may cause short-term disruptions. The Chinese symbol for change is the combination of two words – opportunity and danger. For those of us who have walked this path with a congregation we can say 'Amen' to that!

One of the most conservative institutions in society is the Church. The 'we-never-did-it-that-way-before' syndrome has no doubt been the death knell to many ideas, prevented much progress and no doubt often grieved the Holy Spirit. However conservatism is not always a bad thing. The need to maintain a stable and secure environment in the midst of the rapid change and increasing pressure within society has an important role to play in our lives. As well as this, the major doctrinal tenents of our Christian faith are not negotiable – the trinity, the birth, death and resurrection of Christ, human sin and justification by faith. These must be preserved and are foundational. There are however, many areas in congregational life which can and often should be changed.

Breaking of Bread

For many years our tradition has maintained a particular structure for the Sunday morning service – the Breaking of Bread, or the worship service. Up to the mid 1970's one could go into almost any church like ours in this country at 11.00am on Sunday morning and be sure of being able to participate in the Breaking of Bread service. In such a service there is no formal leadership and men participate in a voluntary manner.

Often such services would follow a particular theme and no doubt when they were first instituted were vital, alive services – a major break from the more structured, liturgical services from which our early founders had been drawn.

Unfortunately many of us remember our Worship services as being fairly predictable and often boring. A favourite pastime for the younger set was the timing of brother so-and-so's prayer, or predicting whether or not we would have Mr X's favourite hymn this morning! We remember that embarrassing morning when the bread slipped off the plate and onto the floor, much to the absolute mortification of the person concerned!

There were, however, the exceptions to the rather dull and predictable mornings and these could be deeply moving services, especially when a new Christian would pour out his heart's gratitude to his Lord and Saviour.

The Sunday morning service was the main congregational activity for the week and absence from it would normally be noted. Several consecutive absences were tantamount to backsliding and would probably elicit a visit from the elders. The centrality of this service in the life of our denomination gave it a very secure place and hallowed feel. Any suggestions of change would bring great consternation within the fellowship. The introduction of an organ or piano to help the singing is still resisted today in some of our churches in this country and many and grievous are the battles that have been fought over this issue.

In the early 1970's the eldership of our congregation had recognised that Sunday morning was a strategic time, both for the family and the community. If people in the community were interested in coming to church, then this was the traditional time they would set aside for this purpose. However the form of service operating in most congregations in our denomination was, to put it mildly, off-putting to strangers; no obvious directed leadership, men randomly popping up around the congregation to make contributions, no worthwhile input for children and often no musical instruments. Sometimes visitors would be asked to sit in the back seats. Those who were not Christians would be asked to refrain from taking the communion.

Such features were hardly calculated to make it a comfortable service for people from the community. It is claimed that from time to time non-Christian people would come into such a service, would be challenged by the simplicity and sincerity of those participating and that this would lead to them coming to faith in Christ. Praise God for every time that this happened although it would be the very occasional exception rather than the rule.

How to change this structure thus permitting a more efficient and effective use of time, has probably been one of the greatest challenges facing congregations in our denomination. Our congregation was no exception!! To even consider any changes seemed to send shock waves through people.

Over the years many discussions were held about the form of the Sunday morning services and many ideas considered. Sometimes it would take up to three or more years from the time an idea was raised until it was implemented.

Initially we held Sunday School at 9.00am followed by the communion service at 11.00am. This often meant that people started their Sunday at 8.00am and would be finishing lunch dishes at 3.00pm. Hardly a day of rest!!

Later we had a Family Service first but then we had to hustle the people from the community out the door, so that we could settle into our communion service. Still later we held a Family service in the morning and a communion service in the evening. This was not very satisfactory as it meant that solo parents with children could not get out and normally only one parent of a family could attend. Finally we moved to one all-in service on Sunday morning and put communion into small groups – which incidentally is where Jesus instituted it in the first place.

One of the stumbling blocks for us in the breaking of bread service had been the linking of worship and communion in the same service. There is no Biblical precedent for this. By separating these two activities it is possible to be much more flexible. We encourage people nowadays to take communion together in home groups, when they entertain visitors for meals, when praying for healing, or for each other and during wedding ceremonies. In fact it can be taken whenever Christians gather together. It was birthed in relationships and should be practised in relationships. What was initially a simple act between the Lord and His disciples has, in many churches, become a ceremonial event. We have found it helpful to have communion available each Sunday at one side of the auditorium so that people can share this together after the service with friends and family if they so desire. There are, of course, both weaknesses and strengths in all of these ways of participating in communion and we would not want to claim that any particular way is better than any other. Maybe having a variety of approaches helps people to maintain something of its freshness and vitality.

Bringing Change

There are two levels from which change can be effected – from leadership and from within the congregation. Each requires different approaches if change is going to occur.

For change to occur smoothly through the leadership taking action we have found the following suggestions helpful.

* **Teach on change**

God is creative and He has built creativity into His people. We have the idea that God is unchanging, perhaps a bit like the Statue of Liberty. Because He is unchanging we will also be unchanging. We have failed to realise that God is unchanging in terms of His character. He is always just, loving, all powerful, all knowing. One of His unchanging characteristics is that He delights in doing new things. The Bible talks about a new creation, a new covenant, new things, a new commandment, a new heaven and earth. All of these are part of God's activity and all indicate change.

* **God's purpose is maturity in individuals and groups**

Maturity by definition means change and is therefore not a threat but an essential part of an individual Christian's life and also an essential part of congregational life.

* **The need for the ministry of the Holy Spirit**

It probably goes without saying that the ministry of the

Holy Spirit and prayer are essential ingredients when changes are being considered.

* *Adequate communication is imperative*

As a congregation gets bigger, communication becomes harder and harder. We must seek out the most effective ways to communicate with the congregation when change is occurring; provide times for discussions and questions, share with key groups, use overheads, drama and other visuals, and provide clear, concise written statements to the congregation. Be persistent, things will need to be said more than once!

* *Use papers to present positions*

Presenting papers for discussion when there is difference of opinion often prevents 'off the cuff' statements and forces people to carefully consider others' points of view.

* *Model whatever the changes are*

Much of Christian life is caught not taught. Leaders should be the first to model the changes which are being sought.

* *Run with the runners*

In any congregation it is estimated that about 2.5% will be innovators. They will create new ideas, absorb them quickly and change rapidly. Another group is the early adapters (about 13.5%). It may take this group up to 6 months to change. Involve these people. They will do a lot of work for the leadership amongst the congregation and reinforce what leadership is saying.

* *Trial it*

Some decisions can be tested before the final action is taken. We have sometimes found that a full assessment by everyone, following a 6 month trial period, can help people adjust to changes.

* *Try questionnaires*

Carefully constructed questionnaires to the congregation with provision for a response often enables the leadership to assess more accurately what people's thinking is about an issue. This also provides an opportunity to objectively inform the congregation as to the support for or against the proposed change. We used this method to assess where our congregation stood on the matter of public participation by women. On discovering that only a very small percentage of people were opposed to this development, the elders were able to visit each of these and talk with them about this matter. Sometimes realising that you are part of a small minority opposing a certain action, may help people accommodate to change or at least not to stand in its way.

* Teach on the area needing change

When we started to move along the path of permitting all the gifts to function in our congregation we taught through 1 Corinthians 12 to 14. Inevitably people will criticise and say that the teaching has become unbalanced because of all this emphasis on "gifts," or whatever the topic may be. It is often necessary to address a previous imbalance on a topic with a temporary imbalance in the new direction.

* Be patient with people

Show love and concern to those who are struggling. Everybody learns at different rates. Some of those in our congregation, once most antagonistic towards the work of the Holy Spirit, are now most involved!

Unfortunately it is sometimes the leadership that is preventing change while members of the congregation are keen to move on into new areas. To achieve change in this situation is much more difficult but not impossible. Lay people finding themselves in such a situation must model, as far as possible, whatever it is they feel needs the change. Timothy was instructed to 'be an example' to others (1 Tim 4:12). It is often helpful to humbly discuss concerns with a sympathetic leader and seek to have input into the situation in this way. Passing on tapes and books to leaders and asking them what they think about the content will sow seeds in their minds. If the area of change does not affect the whole church then those interested should ask for an opportunity to trial whatever it is they feel concerned about.

Recognising people's response to change can often be important. Sometimes the response is fear. What will happen? Where will it lead? These were questions often asked by people in our congregation during discussions on various aspects of the work of the Holy Spirit. Insecurity is another reaction – my secure predictable little world is crumbling. Threatened feelings are often a barrier. When beliefs and strongly held doctrinal positions are threatened this may cause an emotional response. It is very difficult, if not impossible, to counteract an emotional response with logic. Leadership has to be very patient here.

Creating a climate for change rests solely in the court of the leadership; not change for change's sake, but an openness to assess and alter structures, methods and in some cases, as our understanding of God's truth and purposes grows, to alter our position on doctrinal areas.

Balancing enough of the old with the challenge of the new is also a difficult path for leadership to follow. Jesus said new treasures as well as old need to be brought out (Matt 13:52). May God give us all the grace to conserve the good while at the same time pushing on into the new.

CHAPTER
FIVE

REACHING INTO THE COMMUNITY

The congregation was growing. There was a sense of expectancy in the services. We were prepared to try new things. In fact, people commented that no two services seemed to be the same. It was stimulating and we were all very busy. There were new Christians to nurture and they all seemed to have so much to sort out – surely it was easier in the good old days! It hadn't taken us long to discover that it was much easier to catch fish than to clean them!

When a church starts to grow and people get busy, what's the next thing to do? Why, appoint a pastor of course, he can get all that extra work done!

Wrong!

Or at least that's what God seemed to be indicating to this congregation. The leadership of the Chapel sensed that the Lord had something else in mind. Rather than putting our money into a full-time pastor to cater for our own needs we should be considering putting it into a couple who would serve the community and minister to needy people outside the church.

John and Elaine commenced as full-time Christian community workers in 1980. They visited people, painted houses, weeded gardens, took people to the doctor, carried out small home-maintenance requirements, counselled people, did practical work in homes, mowed lawns, cut down trees, had numerous cups of tea and shared their faith.

As a couple they had been through difficult times themselves and were able to sympathise with the needs of others in the community. They were soon to discover that showing genuine concern and care for others created many opportunities to sit down and talk with people. Those they helped wondered how it was that they were not being charged for the service. When they discovered that the salary was contributed by people attending the local church they expressed surprise. In many cases it seemed that their impression of churches was that they were always asking for money – this was different. This was a church giving their money away! Now that's unusual!

During the eighteen months that John and Elaine worked in the community they had the privilege of leading people to the Lord. This was a bonus!

Following their work in the community, an unemployment scheme was launched. This was run by Christians and funded by the Government. For about four years, teams of young people went around the area helping those in need, establishing good work habits in the young people working on the scheme and creating an enormous reservoir of goodwill within the community.

It is important to note that for us, this concern for the needs of people in our community came out of renewal. People's hearts had been touched, there was a compassion and a desire to minister the love of Jesus to them. Some of the best motivation for service and witness comes from a renewing work of the Holy Spirit. It is significant to note that Jesus said that 'the Holy Spirit was upon him' (Luke 4:18) and at least part of that ministry of the Spirit was towards the needy around about him – 'to release the oppressed'.

We were starting to realise that because God was interested in the whole person, we needed to show a sincere interest in the physical and practical needs of those around about us. It was quite the accepted thing for missionaries to go to distant lands to minister to people's educational, health, nutritional, and housing needs, but to do this in our country, a land where the Government had a social policy for its residents from the cradle to the grave, had seemed to escape the notice of many evangelical Christians. Certainly we had not considered it of much importance prior to this.

However, wasn't getting out into the community and helping people with their problems the social gospel? That was only for the 'liberals' and we knew they had gone off the spiritual rails years ago! To be sure there were those troubling verses in Matthew 25 about sheep and goats, people being hungry, thirsty, and naked, and those on the left and the right. These verses couldn't really be for today could they? Jesus clearly says that we were to do this to 'brothers of his.' That must mean these verses applied only to the Jews, not to us. Anyway most of Matthew was for the Jews, so we could ignore it!

The liberals (social gospelers) had parted company with the fundamentalists years ago. The roots of this were in the understanding about the 'depravity of people'. Fundamentalists said that people were totally sinful, utterly rotten and only a saving work of Jesus Christ could change them. The liberals on the other hand said there was much that was good in human beings. They saw hope in the fast growing achievements of the human race, its educational system, its scientific and technological achievements. They had put their hope for this world's salvation in these and in people's basic goodness. Both the liberals and the fundamentalists were only partly right.

Fundamentalists had overlooked the fact that men and women were made in the image of the creator. No matter how sinful a person was, there was still an 'echo' of the creator in every human being on earth. People were capable of noble deeds and thoughts. Liberals, on the other hand, had ignored the great truth of the reformation – *sola gratis, sola fida, sola Christus* – solely by grace, solely by faith, solely by Christ. They had placed too great an emphasis on the ability and goodness of human beings. The brutality of two World Wars was to shatter their dream.

These two different starting points had meant that Fundamentalists had gone for evangelism – to convert souls – and ignored the fact that salvation affected the whole person, while Liberals had gone for social action – to improve life – and had largely ignored the fact of sin and its effects in the lives of people.

Was it just possible that we could combine the strengths of these two positions in a ministry to our community? Could we recognise the dignity, worth and value of individuals and seek to minister in love to their needs and, at the same time bring the message of hope in Christ – that only He could deal with the deepest issues of life? John and Elaine were to show us that this could be done.

Surely if the gospel was really what we claimed it to be, it should impact and affect all aspects of an individual's life and all areas of a society. It had to be a whole gospel.

Sin had penetrated the whole human race and all systems, structures and relationships which men and women had established. If sin had gone that far, then God's saving and healing grace must be capable of reaching this far as well. Human beings were not just souls that needed saving, they were people with hurts and relationships which needed restoring, bodies which often needed healing, finances which needed sorting out and minds which needed a new perspective from which to view life.

It's a hurting community

Over the last few years we have seen a staggering escalation in the burden of hurt within our communities.

Drugs and glue sniffing have permanently damaged minds and bodies of the young and old alike.

Alcohol has destroyed lives, wrecked households, created agony on the roads and put incredible pressures on our welfare state.

Sexual promiscuity and perversion have degraded relationships between men and women, shattered families, debased womanhood, seduced and ensnared young people, blurred the boundaries between male and female and unleashed the deadly Aids epidemic.

The occult and Eastern religions have invaded educational institutions, the welfare services, the medical practice and even Christianity. Objectivity has been reduced to a mere vestige and the latest new Guru, technique or fad is followed mindlessly.

Crime and violence stalk the streets and regularly shatter the lives of those living within what once used to be the safe environment of their home.

Economic pressures and unemployment have reduced the lives of hundreds of people to drudgery and boredom, destroyed self worth and caused an escalation in the suicide rate.

All this, while the advertising man has pandered to our greed, stimulated coveteousness and told us that real living is just around the corner with the next intoxicating purchase. We have more labour-saving devices than any generation that has ever lived on this planet, but less time to do the things that really matter!

These factors are all taking a horrifying cumulative toll on our society, with each generation having a lowered resistance which is measured by deeper emotional scars, psychological problems, confusion, guilt and hurt.

If there was ever a time when people needed to know the grace, power and forgiveness of God, it is now. If there is ever a time when we need Christians filled with the love of Christ, empowered by the Holy Spirit and available to lovingly serve within their communities, it's now.

It is encouraging to see evangelical Christians around the world rising to this challenge and seeking to reach out to those in need around them.

Social dimension of the Gospel

The social dimension of the gospel is not the social gospel. Neither is it socialism nor communism nor any other political agenda. It is simply a genuine concern and compassion within the hearts of Christians for the needs of other people and willingness to sacrifice their own rights and privileges as they seek to reach out and meet those needs.

Social concern reflects the character of God. 'The Maker of heaven and earth ... upholds the oppressed ... gives food to the hungry ... sets prisoners free ... gives sight to the blind ... lifts up those who are bowed down ... watches over the alien ... sustains the fatherless and widow' (Ps 146:5-10). God is a God of justice, mercy, love and compassion. He hates all forms of evil and injustice and has a deep concern for the poor of this planet. If we are genuinely children of the Father then we should be reflecting His qualities and concerns.

Social concern is a divine commandment. 'Seek justice, encourage the oppressed, defend the fatherless, plead for the widow' (Is 1:17). 'Do not forget to do good and share with others for with such sacrifices God is well pleased' (Heb 13:16). 'Command those who are rich in this present world . . . to be rich in good deeds . . . to be generous and willing to share' (1 Tim 6:17-19). Jesus said that the great commandment embraced loving our neighbour as ourself (Lk 10:30-37) and told the parable of the Good Samaritan which powerfully illustrated this point. The Samaritan on his way down from Jerusalem to Jericho reached across the cultural divide – the man he helped was probably a Jew. He reached across the economic divide – the man he helped was poor, stripped and naked. He reached across the physical divide – the man was bloodied, bruised, probably covered with dust and dirt and lying in the gutter. The Samaritan interrupted his schedule and used his time for this man – maybe up to 18 hours (he stayed overnight). The Samaritan used his money (more than two days wages) and possessions (donkey, wine, oil and bandages) for this man. The Samaritan used his abilities (his strength – he lifted him onto the donkey, his skills – he bandaged him, his compassion – he took pity on him) for this man. Love means using our time, possessions and abilities, the only three comodities we have, for others. Jesus says we 'should go and do likewise'. It is a divine command.

Social concern is a fruit of conversion. 'We are saved by grace . . . and created in Christ Jesus for good works' (Eph 2:8-9). We are to 'sow to the Spirit to reap eternal life . . . not to be weary in well doing . . . to do good to all people especially those of the household of faith' (Gal 6:8-9). If we consider ourselves religious we should 'look after orphans and widows' (James 1:27). The fruit of the Spirit is 'love . . . gentleness . . . goodness' (Gal 5:22) and James reminds us that 'faith without deeds is useless' (James 2:20).

Social concern is an evidence of genuine love. Numerous times in the life of Jesus we read that He had compassion on people and in all but one of these times we see Him reaching out to minister to physical need. His compassion led Him to heal people (Matt 14:14, Matt 20:34, Mark 1:41), feed people (Matt 15:32), raise a dead son (Lk 7:13) or seeing people like sheep, harassed and helpless, commission His disciples to go and help them (Matt 9:36 – 10:1). The biblical view of love, God's type of love, is that it is only genuine love if it reaches out to seek to alleviate need. 'This is how we know what love is: Jesus Christ laid down his life for us. We ought to lay down our lives for our brothers. If anyone has material possessions and sees his brother in need but has no pity (same root word as used for the compassion of Jesus) on him, how can the love of God be in him? Dear children, let us not love with words or tongue but with actions and in truth' (1 John 3:16-18).

Social concern may need to embrace social justice. In most cases it is not enough just to have mercy on those in need by seeking to help them; we may also have to address the cause(s) of that need. Such causes may rest with the person in need and if so must be worked through for long term alleviation to occur. Thus people in financial difficulty may require help with budgeting, not just hand outs to help them through. Sometimes the needs that people have may be caused by the injustices of others or the oppressive political or social systems under which people live. God hates injustice (Amos 5:11, 8:5-6, Jer 5:27), so must we His people. Acts of mercy may expose injustice and lead us to confront that injustice. This could be costly but 'everyone who wants to live a godly life in Christ Jesus will be persecuted' (2 Tim 3:12). Proverbs 29:7 says, 'The righteous care about justice for the poor' and Is 11:4 tells us that God will give decisions for the poor of the earth with justice.

Needs people have

It's late Thursday afternoon and we have just received a desperate cry for help from a solo mother with 3 children under five. She is over $300 behind on her electric power bill and the Power Authority says her electricity will be cut off the next day. Social Welfare has been contacted, but the cheque to cover the arrears seems to have got lost somewhere in the pipeline. It's the middle of winter and nappies are piling up. We have had a request to lend her the money so as her power will not be discontinued over the weekend. A simple request you might think, but we have never done this before and we don't even know the woman.

Our evangelical background had conditioned us to see this woman as a soul needing to be saved, but at this moment, salvation from sin was the last thing on her mind. It was within our power to meet this financial need, so clearly, we had a responsibility to consider the request. Much to her relief we lent her the money and a week later she was able to repay it, when the Welfare cheque surfaced. It was then that she asked the questions about why we had lent her this money when we didn't even know her. In turn we were able to share with her about God's love.

Psychologist Abraham Maslow has suggested that all human beings basically have the same set of needs. These needs must be satisfied in a definite order of priority. This has led to an understanding of a hierarchy of needs where the lower or most basic needs must be met first (Fig 2).

Level V. Self actualisation needs. Deprivation – frustration, emptiness, boredom, lack of fulfilment in life.	Basic need – SIGNIFICANCE
Level IV. Success and achievement needs. Deprivation – guilt, embarrassment, inadequacy, lack of self worth / respect	
Level III. Love and affection needs. Deprivation – loneliness, rejection, lack of acceptance or intimacy.	Basic need – BELONGING
Level II. Safety and security needs. Deprivation – threats, anxiety, fears, lack of space, lack of housing.	Basic need – SECURITY
Level I. Physical needs. Deprivation – pain, lack of food, rest, shelter, clothing, health.	

Figure 2. Hierarchy of needs.

Maslow's list of five categories can be reduced to three fundamental human needs. The need for significance, the need to belong and the need for security.

A person facing a physical need such as lack of food is compelled to seek to meet that need first before wanting to discuss life's goals and ambitions or how Jesus can bring them individual fulfilment. An African proverb says this very clearly – 'Empty bellies have no ears.' There is a further illustration of this principle in Exodus 6:9 where the Israelites did not listen to Moses because of their discouragement and cruel bondage.

The woman above, threatened with the cutting off of her electric power (a safety, security need), would not have been interested if the community workers had sat down with her to share the gospel, ignoring the serious situation which she was facing.

Christians have to *be* the good news before they have the right to *speak* the good news.

The good news is that the gospel addresses all the various needs that human beings face. If it is a security need then God can provide this, often through His people. If it is a belonging need, then God offers His love and companionship, and again, this may come through Christians. If it is significance that a person is seeking, then Christian faith provides this. God has an intense interest in each individual. Each person is unique and can find forgiveness, purpose, and relevance in God.

We best minister to people facing needs of security by *serving* them as Jesus would have done, as with the illustration above of the lady unable to pay the power bill; those facing needs of belonging, by *loving* them for Jesus' sake; those facing needs related to significance, by *telling* of God's plan of salvation for human beings. All too often evangelicals have started by *telling*, while totally disregarding the person's current situation. By doing this we have often been accused of being irrelevant or 'scratching where a person is not itching.' 'Telling' has a place in evangelism but it may not be the first place.

Credibility – a crisis for the Church

Over the past few years it seems as if the credibility of the Church has hit an all-time low. Not only do people within society see the Church as some sort of dinosaur – a relic of some by-gone age, but many people within the Church are also questioning its validity. Somewhere, we seem to have lost it. To ask what perception the local community has of our church may produce an embarrassing answer, but it might put us on the way to dealing with a credibility crisis.

Some people's view of the Church is that of the TV image – a sort of old people's club, tea parties and bumbling parsons. For others it is of a weird group of people swinging from the chandeliers – they picture Jonestown Guyana, may link it with some of the sects or, more recently, the TV evangelists. Many people see the Church as a group of narrow, bigoted, do-gooders whose one aim in life is to restrict what people can do and make others unhappy. In some cases people just don't know what goes on in churches. They've never been inside one and they have no desire to do so either. They probably have as much interest in the Church as the average Christian would have in the Masonic Lodge down the road. Some people used to go to church, but what they experienced was thoroughly predictable and totally irrelevant to the twentieth century. They soon found other ways to spend their time more profitably. Many people are put off the Church and therefore Christianity because of the numerous denominations and divisions they see. It genuinely confuses them and hence they have an easy excuse for non involvement.

The credibility of the modern Church is markedly different from that of the early Church. We read that the community was 'filled with awe' (Acts 2:43), that the Church 'enjoyed the good will of all people' (Acts 2:47). People were surprised and amazed at what happened (Acts 3:10). The Church 'frightened' the religious leaders of the day (Acts 4:17) and the 'people were all praising God' (Acts 4:21). At one stage 'nobody dared to join them' and 'people spoke highly of them' (Acts 5:13). On another occasion the 'officers didn't use force . . . they were frightened the people might stone them' (Acts 5:26). The Church was obviously highly credible, influencing all areas of the community and thoroughly relevant.

How can the modern Church regain credibility? Will it come by constructing big church buildings? What about changing our services or brightening up our singing? Perhaps the answer is in big evangelistic rallies? How about successful TV shows, Christian Disneylands or high profile ministries? Some of these things may help a little but they are not the ways that the Church should seek to gain credibility. The world can normally do all of these things much better than we in the Church, they generally have greater access to the media and have more money than the Church.

There is an avenue left to the Christian Church. It is the avenue of servanthood. Credibility is primarily gained by lovingly and sacrificially serving other people. In an age of hedonistic self-indulgence, this is not popular. Neither does it offer a quick fix for a broken society or excitement, glamour and instant success for the Church – it is a ministry which demands the long haul. The heart of the three years of the ministry of Jesus was essentially this – serving others. 'The Son of Man did not come to be served but to serve' (Matt 20:25-28).

Unfortunately the modern Church is normally far removed from serving the hurting community. Many evangelicals have left that aspect to the Salvation Army – 'We're here to win souls and evangelise,' is a common conception. In place of the Church, the humanists have manned the social concern agencies and support services. It is normally the feminists who run the homes for battered wives. All too often Christians are seen as legalistic, cold, uncompassionate people. People who are only too willing to tell others how to live their lives but are not willing to get involved with the deep needs of their community.

They are seen as people who stand aloof from others, and convey a 'holier than thou' attitude, prepared to condemn homosexuality but not minister to the needs of the homosexual.

For the last 20 years, one of the most credible witnesses to Christ has been a frail little nun, living a simple lifestyle among the poor in Calcutta. Mother Teresa has captured the hearts of Christian and non-christian, rich and poor, powerful and weak, East and West, with her compassion and servant heart for the dying of Calcutta. One doesn't build a church by ministering to the dying. There is not much future for such people. They will not be able to contribute to growth statistics, building programmes, dynamic celebration services or evangelistic outreaches. Such a strategy (ministering to the dying) is not high on the list of Church growth strategies but I am absolutely sure that it is on God's heart.

Church leaders and congregations must explore and recapture this dimension of Christianity if we are to take the high ground and again become relevant and effective in our communities.

CHAPTER SIX

WORDS, DEEDS AND SIGNS

I remember when a team of us were keen to share the Gospel. We were in our teens or early twenties and lived in a small country town. It was a Sunday afternoon and we were busily setting up our amplification on the road side. The sun was shining. The cows and sheep grazed quietly in the fields and people were travelling to and fro along the road in their cars enjoying a quiet Sunday afternoon outing.

That afternoon we shared our testimonies, somebody gave a gospel address and we played Christian music. I cannot remember anyone actually stopping to listen. Certainly we didn't speak to anybody. The people in the cars continued on their Sunday afternoon jaunts with only a quizzical sideways-look as they passed by and the cows and sheep showed not the slightest interest at all in what we were doing! However, we returned home happy with the fact that we had preached the gospel. It probably did nothing for those who had maybe caught a few words as they passed, but it had made us feel very good.

The need for words

Evangelism by words was my heritage. As young people we were encouraged to share our faith with friends, to preach in the 'open air' or at the beach and were given opportunities to speak at the 7.00pm Sunday 'gospel service' to the Christians who faithfully attended. There was nothing wrong with this.

Part of the great commission was to preach and teach but we were to discover that it was not the only way to present the gospel.

Churches have never had any problem in recognising the need for a verbal declaration of the truth. Pulpits and seating arrangements in Church buildings bear silent testimony to the emphasis we place on this aspect of proclaiming the gospel. The Christian Church has employed literature and radio ministries very successfully during much of the twentieth century and this has led to many thousands of people coming to faith in Christ. Since its inception our congregation has also employed this means of evangelism effectively. We have run missions, organised youth outreaches, visited door to door around our church, used films as an evangelistic tool and had letter box drops from time to time to our local community. All of these have resulted in a few people coming to faith in Christ.

Many of those who came to faith through our congregation during the 1980's came as a result of their friends or family members sharing their new found faith with them. Evangelism by word just happened. The changes in the lives of new Christians caused others to ask questions about what had occurred and this lead to the opportunity to talk about Christ to those wanting to know.

The need for deeds

The effect of releasing community workers into our local community has shown us that we can also proclaim the gospel by deed. This is often an effective way into a person's heart.

We discovered that there were numerous verses in the New Testament speaking about the importance of 'good works'. Good works 'would glorify the Father' (Matt 5:16). 'God gives generously . . . so we can abound to every good work' (2 Cor 9:8). We are commanded to 'do good to everyone, especially those of the household of faith' (Gal 6:10). 'It is to be our aim to do good to one another' (1 Thess 5:15). Titus was encouraged to 'show himself a pattern of good works' (Tit 2:7), 'to be ready to do every good work' (Tit 3:1) and to 'maintain good works' (Tit 3:14). We are to 'provoke one another to love and good works' (Heb 10:24) and so on. But being brought up in an evangelical church the thought of 'good works' sent a repulsive shiver down one's back. In seeking to uphold salvation by grace, through faith and not by works (Eph 2:8) we had come to think of good works as bad works! Many was the time that I had heard the gospel preached from Ephesians 2:8 and been told in no uncertain terms that good works could never earn a person their salvation. In fact, all our works were just like filthy rags in God's sight (Is 64:6). However, I can not remember hearing Eph 2:9 read in this context – 'We are God's workmanship, created in Christ Jesus to good works, which God prepared in advance for us to do.' It was quite a shock for me to discover some years later that these two verses were in such close proximity to each other. Certainly it is true that we cannot *attain* our salvation by doing good works. However we were to discover that doing good works to others may help them *obtain* theirs.

The need for signs

One evening a lady in the congregation brought an eight month old baby to a home group because she did not have baby sitters for the evening. During the evening it came to the attention of the group that the baby had had conjunctivitis from the day of birth. Each morning the mother had to spend time seeking to separate the child's eyelids when the baby awoke. That night people gathered around, laid hands on the child and prayed for its healing. Next morning the baby awoke with clear eyes, completely healed. The father of the child was not a Christian. In fact, he was an alcoholic and the family had been under a great deal of stress. The miracle of the healing of his baby boy and other factors were to bring him to Christ within a few weeks of that event.

In another instance a member of the congregation got to talking to a young lady in a shop next door to where she was working. This young lady and her friend were living in de facto relationships with their boyfriends in a flat. That day she recounted how several unusual and inexplicable things had been happening at night. Doors had been slamming and windows closing for no apparent reason. These four young people had become very frightened and, what's more, a German Shepherd dog which they kept, had also become terrified and had bounded straight out through a window during one of these evenings. This seemed to be a clear case of occult activity. It was arranged for two men from the congregation to go around to the house and they prayed through it, claiming the authority of God in this home. From that evening on there were no further unusual occurrences. Within a few months of that event one couple came to the Lord and were married. It is in the purposes of God for His people to experience the authoritative demonstration of His power from time to time, as a sign of His living presence among His people.

Paul, talking about his ministry, tells about the 'demonstration of the Spirit and of power' (1 Cor 2:4) and 'mighty signs and wonders, by the power of the Spirit' (Rom 15:19). Such evidences of God's power were manifest in the life of Christ, the early Church and the lives of the Apostles. Jesus, speaking about His miracles as an evidence of the relationship He had with the Father, says that those who believed in Him would do greater things than these (John 14:10-12).

The gospel is proclaimed whenever the power of God confronts and overcomes either the effects of sin in people's lives or directly impacts Satanic authorities. The new birth, a healing, a miraculous intervention in a hopeless situation, the freeing from demonic activity are all evidences of the *dunamis* (power) of God at work in human lives because of the resurrection of Jesus Christ from the dead.

The need for balance

As we look across the Body of Christ today we see various groups or denominations who tend to emphasise one of these three methods of presenting the gospel.

Conservative evangelical churches have tended to emphasise *words* more than deeds or signs. Some Pentecostal or Charismatic groups have placed greater emphasis on *signs*, while more liberal groups have tended to be more concerned about social justice and good works – the *deeds* aspect of the gospel. Not only this, but each group has tended to see their emphasis as the most important and in some cases as the only legitimate emphasis.

In the ministry of Jesus we see a perfect balance in His presentation of the gospel. We read that Jesus 'preached peace' (words). He was anointed with the Holy Ghost and power ... healing all that were oppressed by the devil' (signs) and that He went about 'doing good' (deeds) (Acts 10:36-38).

In the synagogue He read from the prophecy of Isaiah which said He was to 'preach the gospel to the poor' (words), 'to heal and deliver' (signs) and to 'set at liberty them that are bruised' (Luke 4:18-19). This last phrase can be translated 'lift the burden from the downtrodden' (deeds).

In the Lord's ministry we see a full-orbed proclamation of the gospel. He fed people. He healed people. He preached to crowds. He spoke to individuals. He ministered to children. He confronted the powers of darkness and demanded that they yield to His authority.

In the life of the early Church we again see this threefold presentation. The early Christians preached and spoke (Acts 2:14, 4:2, 6:10); they saw evidence of the power of God among them (Acts 2:43, 5:11) and there was the obvious concern for people's practical needs and the demonstration of Christian love (Acts 2:44-45, 6:1-4) – words, deeds and signs.

Similarly Paul could say that what Christ had accomplished in him had been done 'by words and deeds, by the power of signs and miracles, and by the power of the Spirit' (Rom 15:18-19).

Word, Deed and Sign gifts

The Holy Spirit has maintained this same balance in the distribution of gifts to the Body of Christ. There are 'word' gifts – teaching, exhortation and evangelism (Rom 12:7-8). There are 'deed' gifts – serving, giving, acts of mercy, helps (Rom 12:7-8, 1 Cor 12:28) and there are 'sign' gifts – healings, miracles and faith (1 Cor 12:9-10).

Our observation is that individual believers will often have a marked orientation towards one of these three ways of presenting the gospel. There are those whose ministry is clearly that of the spoken word. They are comfortable in this and there is obvious fruit in their ministry. Others have a deed-orientated ministry. This is often expressed in a deep compassion for people experiencing injustice and concern for the poor. Such people will normally give themselves to those in need, actively serving those around them.

Then there are those who seem to have a special interest and ability when it comes to confronting Satanic authorities, praying for healing, or in other areas where an authoritative demonstration of the power of God is needed.

Unfortunately, many mainline conservative churches have shown a marked disinterest in, even hostility to, this latter aspect of the presentation of the gospel. As members of their congregations have sought to investigate the area of signs or sensed God's touch on them in gifting by His Spirit, they have been met with fear and suspicion. Instead of being encouraged and given biblical guidelines for the expression of this God-given authority, they have often been rejected or neglected. Many have been forced to find other fellowships which were open to such areas.

Words proclaim the *truth* about God, deeds show the love of God and signs demonstrate the *power* of God. Surely if Jesus employed this threefold proclamation of the gospel, then doesn't the Church, His Body, need to as well?

To rely on words alone means that we are competing against all the philosophies, ideas and theories of secular and religious people. To rely on deeds alone means we simply compete with the wide variety of humanistic aid and charitable organisations in society. To rely on signs alone brings us into direct competition with Satanic counterfeits. We see an example of Satanic counterfeit when Moses was opposed by the magicians of Egypt (Ex 7:7-10).

The Lausanne Congress for evangelism, in 1974, was the springboard for modern evangelicals to consider the need for social concern and this congress linked words and deeds. Lausanne II, in 1989, confronted the modern evangelical world with the miraculous and its impact for the gospel around the world, thus linking signs to words and deeds. To present the whole gospel surely means that we must be open to these three dimensions.

As a congregation we have attempted to explore these three dimensions. Coming from an evangelical heritage we were committed to words. Moving into renewal, we have experienced something of signs and from there we have sensed God's call regarding social concern, deeds. We have sought to encourage and equip people to minister in the areas of words, deeds and signs. When such ministries have not been part of our own fellowship or upbringing, we have sought to learn from others and have promoted training sessions, courses and seminars held by those who were experienced in these areas. In some cases finance has been made available to those who could not afford to go to such sessions.

We must strive for balance between these three dimensions of presenting the gospel in our congregations. Scripture tells us that 'a threefold cord is not easily broken' (Ecc 4:12). We need people who are empowered by the Holy Spirit, motivated by the love of Christ, with a heart of compassion for a hurting society and able to share the Gospel with people at the appropriate moment. We must allow the Holy Spirit to show us creative ways to express this as we seek to impact our communities for Christ.

Watch the new breed of Church that God is seeking to establish. Churches who have experienced renewal and know how to move in the power of the Holy Spirit. Churches that are committed to social concern and reaching out to a broken community with the love and compassion of Christ, seeking to meet the needs of those around, and churches that will also link these two dimensions with a strong commitment to evangelism. Such churches will certainly impact their local communities.

SUMMARY

	EVANGELISM	MIRACULOUS	SOCIAL CONCERN
GOSPEL BY	Words	Signs(Wonders)	Deeds(Works)
PROCLAIMS	Truth of God	Power of God	Love of God
CHURCH STREAM	Evangelicals	Pentecostals/ Charismatics	Liberals
FULFILLED IN JESUS Luke 4:18-19 .... Acts 10:36-38	*Preach the gospel.* .... *the message ... telling the good news.*	*The Spirit of the Lord upon me.* .... *annointed with the Holy Spirit and power ... healing.*	*To the poor. Oppressed.* .... *went around doing good.*

CHAPTER
SEVEN

WANTED – UNIFYING THEME

Why is it that Christians are divided over so many aspects of God's truth? Is it, as Paul says, that differences have to be among us to show who has God's approval (1 Cor 11:18-19)? Or is it due to the fact that we come from different backgrounds and traditions and have been taught different emphases? Could it be because of our different giftings? An evangelist will often see things very differently from the way that a teacher or pastor views things. Perhaps it's just plain stubbornness, pride and ignorance. Or is it a combination of all of these things? Whatever the answer, differences within the Christian community over many issues have caused a great deal of bitterness, much waste of time in argument, needless discussion and serious divisions in the Body of Christ. It has also often brought a lot of shame and scorn on the name of Christ from those outside the Church. David Watson used to say, 'Denominationalism is a stench in the nostrils of the world and keeps them from Christ.'

During the time of tension in our congregation, discussions on the gifts of the Holy Spirit inevitably led to someone reminding us that if a person spoke in tongues and didn't have love, it was worthless (1 Cor 13:1). Nobody could argue about that, it is obviously true. Love must be the central quality of a Christian's life. But if love was lacking it did not mean that tongues were unimportant and could be dismissed, as some people seemed to want to do. Surely a person could speak in tongues and have love at the same time? In our circles, it sometimes seemed that if someone could make a case for the fruit of the Spirit being more important than the gifts of the Spirit, then the gifts could be dismissed altogether.

Another area where there have been lengthy discussions

in the evangelical church, is whether social concern or evangelism should have the highest priority. Still another is the priority of worship over witness. How many of these squabbles are generated by the fact that we were just defending our own understanding, tradition or maybe our own gifting and ministry? Is it really necessary to prioritise these issues? Surely all these various dimensions are important. To try to rank them in order of importance is pointless, to dismiss one at the expense of another leads into error and to argue over them is the height of foolishness.

The discussion on spiritual gifts in 1 Corinthians 12 seems to give us some clues as to how we should deal with important, yet dissimilar issues. If we had to choose between losing our head or a foot, or an eye or a hand (v21), then we would most probably choose to give up a foot before our head and a hand before an eye. After all there is no doubt that you can not do much without a head! But this chapter makes it clear that one part of the body is not more important than another. We are not to prioritise parts of the body, all parts are necessary for a healthy and functional body. Paul uses this argument to point out that one gift is not more important than another. All are necessary in the Church.

This illustration of the body in 1 Corinthians 12 can also be applied to arguments about the relative importance of the gifts of the Spirit over the fruit of the Holy Spirit, or whether evangelism takes priority over social concern. It is not a matter of trying to evaluate which one of these aspects is more important than another. Each is a facet of God's truth, is different and fulfils a different role. Had the Christian Church seen this point we might have prevented many problems, arguments and divisions which have plagued the Body of Christ over the centuries.

As our congregation worked through these various issues, we came to see that providing opportunities for people to develop in all areas they felt God was calling them into, was much more urgent than discussing which area had the highest priority. God has given people different interests, ministries, emphases and giftings. In many cases, all that is necessary is to structure congregational life in such a way that all of these can be utilised.

We saw people working in the community, while others found their place in the ministry of intercession or in leading a homegroup. Some were concerned about political issues, others were called to minister overseas. People were being counselled, spiritual gifts were in evidence. Certain people felt called particularly to the poor, others to the pastoral care of people. Some sensed God's call towards the healing ministry and others got involved in deliverance. There were those who felt God wanted them in the full-time ministry, others sought to use their professional skills or trades to the glory of God. A great variety of ministries and a diverse range of giftings and interests were being released.

However with such a plethora of things happening and the wide range of people's involvement, there still seemed to be something missing; a bigger picture, an over-arching theme or framework.

To be sure, we must place Christ central to all we do, whether that be evangelism, social concern, work, spiritual warfare, service, worship or in the use of the gifts of the Spirit. But to what end result?

Slowly the bigger picture came into focus, as if the pieces of a jigsaw puzzle were finally coming together giving us a total view, a unifying theme. This theme was the KINGDOM OF GOD.

Viewing things from the perspective of the Kingdom of God has enabled us to integrate all that we have seen develop. No longer do we need to debate whether evangelism should take precedence over social concern. Both were an integral part of the Kingdom of God and had to be addressed. No longer were we dealing with a number of disjointed aspects of God's truth. We have been able to see them as a unit, a whole. They were all part of God's agenda for this planet. That agenda is the re-establishment of His Kingdom rule in the lives of human beings and in human society. Social concern, evangelism, spiritual gifts, ministry to the poor, spiritual warfare, making disciples, are all necessary if we are to participate fully in God's agenda.

The issue was not one of priority of one aspect over another, but rather one of emphasis. The greatest challenge for the leadership of any congregation is to seek an effective and harmonious balance between the many different aspects pertaining to the Kingdom of God. We needed to express our theology of these matters in terms of an integrated and practical whole.

The outstanding example of this was of course the life of Jesus Christ. His life demonstrated that balance as He spent time in prayer, taught His disciples, preached to the crowds, came against demonic forces, ministered to the poor.

KINGDOM OF GOD

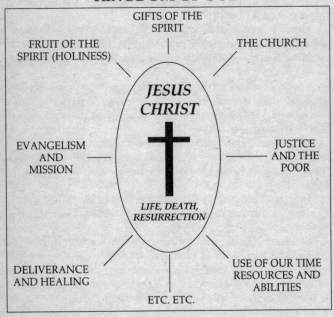

Figure 3. Integrating theme of the Kingdom of God.

One of the purposes of God is to bring all things together in Christ (Eph 1:10). As human beings, we sometimes find it difficult to hold several areas of God's truth together at the same time. By looking at things through 'Kingdom eyes', and keeping Christ central, we have a framework in which to hold the many dimensions of the work of God together in a creative, interactive tension. (See Figure 3)

The Psalmist had grasped something of the greatness of this theme of the Kingdom of God when he wrote,

'All you have made will praise you O Lord; your saints will extol you. They will tell of the glory of your Kingdom and speak of your might so that all men may know of your mighty acts and the glorious splendour of your Kingdom. Your Kingdom is an everlasting Kingdom, and your dominion endures through all generations.' (Ps 145:10-14)

The discovery of the theme of the Kingdom of God was for me, a quantum step forward. It is to this integrating theme of the Kingdom of God that we will now turn our attention.

PART II
BEYOND RENEWAL

CHAPTER
EIGHT

THE KINGDOM OF GOD

We were talking together after a meeting of Church leaders, a fellow pastor and myself. Our conversation had covered several areas of common interest and we had got around to discussing the Kingdom of God. Clearly my friend was somewhat uncomfortable with the topic and finally blurted out, 'All this talk about the Kingdom. I believe the Church is the Kingdom of God!'

For me his remark typified much of the confusion and ignorance about the Kingdom of God which has been evident in the evangelical church over much of this last century. Dispensationalists have said that the Kingdom is still to come and is not currently present. With their view that certain gifts of the Holy Spirit are not present today, they are guilty of relegating areas of the ministry of the Holy Spirit to the past and much of Christ's teaching on the Kingdom of God to the future. This leaves a big hole in the New Testament! More recently, Reconstructionists have urged us to seek to bring in God's Kingdom here and now. By basing all we do on Old Testament law we will be able to fully establish the Kingdom of God and so usher in the return of Christ. Still others have been confused and equated the Church with the Kingdom, as my pastor friend did.

The last few years have seen a literal explosion of teaching of the Kingdom of God right around the world. This is not some new fad but a genuine recovery of the priority of Jesus' teaching and the centrality of the gospel. It would be correct to say that to fully understand the gospel, one must understand the Kingdom of God.

The Kingdom - God's priority

The Kingdom of God is a unifying theme for the whole of Scripture. We can not say it is the main theme. The main theme is the revelation of the character of God Himself. Since the fall God's intention has been to both demonstrate and extend His rule in human beings. His purpose has been to have a person (or people) who would both model to those around them what it was like to live under His rule and seek to extend that rule into the lives of others.

Abraham

God chose Abraham who was 'a stranger in a foreign land' (Heb 11:9) to live by faith under His direction. His intention was to make Abraham's name great and to bless all the peoples of the earth through him (Gen 12:2-3). We see here God's twin purpose of demonstrating His grace and goodness through Abraham and extending His ways through the patriarch to other men and women.

Israel

He raised up the nation of Israel as a people who would demonstrate what it was like to live under His authority. About His decrees and laws God said, 'Observe them carefully, for this will show your wisdom and understanding to the nations, who will hear about all these decrees and say, "Surely this great nation is a wise and understanding people." What other nation is so great as to have their gods near them the way the Lord our God is near us whenever we pray to him?' Deut 4:6-7.

We see God's concern about extending His rule to others through the nation of Israel by provision for those who were not Israelites, the strangers and aliens. His desire was for them to enjoy the provisions of His rule in their lives. In Matthew 23:13-15 we read that the Pharisees were seeking to extend God's rule into the lives of others but this activity had unfortunately gone well astray. Through their misunderstanding and distorting of the ways of God they were making converts that were twice as much sons of hell as they were.

The Church

Then God established the Church. The members of His body were to be colonizers of heaven (Phil 3:20). They were to have their own identity, be clearly recognisable and reflect the features of another society – the society of the Kingdom of God. In this way they would demonstrate to a watching world the values of the Kingdom of God. As well as this, they were commanded by Christ to go into all the world and preach the gospel, thus extending the rule of God into the lives of others also. Philip preached the good news of the Kingdom of God in Samaria (Acts 8:12), Paul argued persuasively about the Kingdom of God in the synagogue in Ephesus (Acts 19:8) and preached it in Rome (Acts 28:31).

So it is for the followers of Jesus today. We are to demonstrate His rule in our lives and so bring the perspective of His truth into all we do and seek to extend the Kingdom of God into the lives of those around about us.

Annie met a young Malaysian girl at a bus stop who was very lonely. The young lady had been in the city for three weeks and knew no one. She chatted to her and arranged to meet with her again. Over the next few weeks Annie, and her husband Ray, showed her around the city, invited her to their home and out to meals. The young lady, a Buddhist, was deeply touched and couldn't understand how it was that Ray and Annie loved her so much. They were able to share their faith with her and lead her to the Lord. She was later baptised and subsequently served the Lord by working among disadvantaged young people.

In Mark 12:29-30 we read the following discussion between Jesus and a teacher of the law.

> Teacher of the law to Jesus: 'Which is the most important commandment?'
> Jesus: 'Love the Lord your God with all your heart and with all your soul and with all your strength and love your neighbour as yourself.'
> Teacher of the law: 'Well said, you are right to say this.'
> Jesus: 'You are not far from the Kingdom of God.'

The teacher of the law understood that love was the

heartbeat of the Kingdom of God. To understand and obey this command is the highest calling a human being can have on this planet. Ray and Annie first demonstrated this aspect of the Kingdom of God to that lonely young Buddhist lady, later they were able to extend that Kingdom rule of God into her life.

The Kingdom - what is it?

Nowhere in Scripture is the Kingdom of God as such, clearly defined for us. Probably the closest we get to a definition is in our Lord's prayer where He prays 'Your Kingdom come, your will be done, on earth as it is in heaven' (Matt 6:10). We understand from this that where the will of God is being done the Kingdom of God is being demonstrated. The Kingdom of God is seen when the will of God is being done. Jesus said that there was no doubt about this occurring in heaven. It is on earth where the Kingdom of God has yet to be fully seen. Thus we can define the Kingdom of God in terms of the Father – where His will is done or His rule is being seen.

Jesus' constant desire was to do the will of the Father (John 5:30). He could say that it was a delight to do the Father's will and He only did those things that pleased the Father. In this way He demonstrated the Kingdom of God in all He did and said.

We can also define the Kingdom of God in terms of the Son. The phrase 'Kingdom of God' occurs less frequently in Acts and the Epistles than it does in the Gospels. However, a similar concept in Acts and the Epistles is that of the Lordship of Jesus. Where Jesus Christ is Lord and Master there the will of God is being done and the Kingdom of God is being manifested.

Finally we can define the Kingdom of God in terms of the Spirit. Jesus said, 'If I drive out demons by the Spirit of God then the Kingdom of God has come among you' (Matt 12:28). The Kingdom of God is evidenced through the ministry of the Holy Spirit. It was the anointing of Jesus by the Spirit which enabled Him to bring the good news of the Kingdom (Luke 4:18). Similarly it was the descent of the Spirit at Pentecost upon the disciples which brought them into the dynamics of the Kingdom of God.

Thus the Kingdom of God can be described in terms of a reign and a realm. Describing it as a reign implies that the Kingdom of God is an activity, an activity involving the rule and authority of God – Father, Son and Spirit – throughout the whole of creation. Describing God's Kingdom as a realm implies the extent of that rule. Its realm is – obedient creation. Some have further defined the Kingdom of God as creation healed and restored. This gives us an even greater appreciation of its scope and extent.

In a practical sense, applying the Kingdom of God to everyday life, each Christian needs to place the whole of their life within the will of the Father, under the Lordship of Christ and seek to live by the power of the Spirit. In this way we will be 'seeking first the Kingdom of God' (Matt 6:33).

Jesus said, 'My Kingdom is not of this world. If it were, then would my servants fight' (John 18:36). The Kingdom of God transcends the world's systems; political, military, legal, educational and financial.

A couple in the congregation who owned a T-shirt shop, had come to faith in Christ and seen a ministry commence among street kids. To enable them to give more time to the young people they were contacting, Ian took over the managing of the T-shirt shop. He believed that God wanted him to move it from its current rather unfavorable position at the top end of the main shopping street, to a position further down the street in a more upmarket position. However, to get a location there was very difficult and extremely expensive. Much prayer and some fasting was made about this matter and several possible locations were explored. Finally one was found that seemed suitable but the previous tenant was asking $45,000 for 'key money'. There was no possible way that the business could afford this amount, so rather than seeking to haggle and reduce the amount, further prayer and fasting was undertaken.

Returning to the previous tenant a few weeks later, Ian found that he had not been able to re-lease the property and he had reduced his key money to $30,000. This was still far too much, so it was turned down. Still the premises were not let. After several further inquiries Ian finally obtained the for $1,000 key money! A reduction of $44,000 in a competitive market for a prime site. 'If it were, my servants would fight . . .' (John 18:36). Most certainly Jesus was not talking about economics here but rather about the use of physical force to prevent His arrest. However, perhaps there are other areas where His servants do not need to fight if they are seeking to achieve the purposes of His Kingdom. Maybe one of these is in the business field. (Note – this shop closed sometime later due to several problems but this in no way takes away from the fact God honoured the prayer and faith of those who set it up.)

We also read that 'the Kingdom of God is not a matter of eating or drinking, but righteousness, joy and peace in the Holy Spirit' (Romans 14:17). It transcends the physical world. It's more a matter of values, qualities of character and authority against Satan and sin.

For quite a while Glen had been concerned about a previous event in his life. While at Intermediate school, aged 12, he had been a monitor in the tuck shop. Frequently he had undercharged or handed out free ice creams, drinks and pies to his friends. Now in his early twenties he was troubled about this. Finally he plucked up enough courage to return to his old school and handed to the new headmaster a cheque for $100 explaining what he had done while he was a tuck shop monitor.

You can imagine the surprise of the headmaster. He was so impressed at what Glen had just done, that he invited him to tell the whole school at the assembly, the following week! There were a few strange looks from the staff as Glen explained the circumstances of the $100 cheque to children who gathered at that assembly.

Living righteously is a mark of a Kingdom person. Righteous living leads to peace in the heart. Peace in the heart leads to joy. The order of these three words in this verse is particularly significant.

Nor is it in 'word but in power' (1 Cor 4:20). It transcends human communication. It is not just ideas, theories, statements or hypotheses.

A sixth form girl had come into a guidance counsellor's study in a State Secondary school. She had had very little sleep each night for some weeks and this had been seriously affecting her school work.

As the counsellor talked with the girl he sensed that there was some occult influence affecting her and so he asked her if she had ever been involved with the occult. She said she had not, so it was back to square one! But again he sensed there was something here that was important. He further sensed that God was saying that she had a book on her bookshelf in her room at home that she needed to get rid of. He even 'knew' where the bookshelf was in her room and what the book was! He mentioned this to the girl and she recognised the book.

On her arrival home the girl removed the occult book from her bookshelf, took it outside, burned it, lay down on her bed at 4.00pm in the afternoon and slept right through till 8.00am next morning!

'The Kingdom of God is not a matter of talk but of power'. If there is one thing that goes on in a Guidance Counsellor's study it is talk! But sometimes talk isn't enough, we need power, the power of the Kingdom of God. The Kingdom of God is more than just the inner reign of Christ in a believer's life. Jesus demonstrated that there was a public dimension to the Kingdom of God by casting out demons, feeding the hungry, healing the sick and raising the dead.

The Kingdom – the ministry of Jesus

From the time of the fall, God's plan was to demonstrate and extend His rule in Old Testament times through His people. To a limited extent this occurred. However it is particularly in the New Testament and especially in the life of Jesus that we discover a fresh and fuller revelation of His Kingdom and see these same two aspects of demonstration and extension of the Kingdom of God in His life, as we saw in Abraham, Israel and the Church.

God sent Jesus who demonstrated perfectly what it was like to live under His authority. The Lord's quality of life, shown by His love, forgiveness, kindness, justice, holiness and servanthood modelled the lifestyle of the Kingdom.

Jesus also sought to extend that Kingdom of the Father as He came against sin, Satan, demons, disease and death, all evidences of the kingdom of darkness, and forced them to retreat. A further aspect of this ministry of extension of God's Kingdom by Jesus is seen in His teaching. Here He sought to extend people's perception and understanding of the Kingdom of God.

He used the illustration of light and salt to describe the influence His followers should have on the surrounding society. Light incorporates the idea of showing the way – demonstration, whereas salt suggests the idea of penetration and preservation – extension.

An interesting Old Testament event gives us some vital clues regarding the timing of this new dimension of God's Kingdom rule on this planet.

In Daniel chapter 2 we read about the dream of Nebuchadnezzar in which he saw a huge statue with head of gold, chest and arms of silver, belly and thighs of brass, legs of iron and feet of iron and clay. In the dream, the statue is destroyed by a rock hewn out of the mountain without the use of human hands. Daniel interprets this dream by explaining that the various metals that made up the statue represent human kingdoms. History records these as the Babylonian (gold), the Medes and Persians (silver), the Grecian (bronze) and the Roman (iron/clay). Each metal has diminishing value and indicates that each successive kingdom would be less splendid. But at the same time each metal has growing toughness, indicating that each kingdom would last longer than the previous one. History reveals that such was the case. The significant verse in this passage is v44 where we read, 'In the times of these kings, the God of heaven will set up a kingdom that will never be destroyed'. Here we have a clear indication of a specific time in history when God was going to establish His Kingdom and this points to the time of Christ. Christ is also the rock hewn out of the mountain. We read that this coming kingdom would be left to another people (handed over to the saints Dan 7:18,27), and would endure forever (v44). The permanence of this kingdom is stressed several times in Daniel (see 4:3,34, 6:26, 7:14,18,).

This prophetic dream leaves us in very little doubt about God's intentions which seem to focus onto the period of the world's history around the time of the life of Christ.

We gain a further clue regarding the timing of this new

dimension of God's Kingdom from Isaiah 9:6-7 where we read, 'For to us a child is born . . . the government will be on his shoulders . . . of the increase of his government and peace there will be no end . . . and he will reign . . . over his kingdom . . . from that time on and forever.' Again we have a clear reference to a kingdom (government) and there is a striking similarity with the idea of permanence which we read of in Daniel.

The fulfilment of the Isaiah 9 passage is found in Luke 1:30-33 where the angel says to Mary, 'You will be with child . . . God will give him a throne . . . he will reign for ever . . . his kingdom will never end.'

As we link all these passages together we are left with the inescapable conclusion that God was about to inaugurate a new dimension of His Kingdom rule on earth and this was to be linked to the ministry of Jesus.

As the forerunner of Jesus, John the Baptist announced that the Kingdom of God was at hand as he preached to the crowds that flocked to hear him saying, 'Repent, for the Kingdom of Heaven is near' (Matt 3:2).

The specific point of the inauguration of the new age of the Kingdom of God seems to be at the time of Christ's baptism when the Holy Spirit descended on Him. He says in Luke 4:18 that He was annointed by the Spirit to preach the gospel to the poor. This gospel to the poor was the gospel of the Kingdom.

There is no doubt about the centrality of the theme of the Kingdom of God in Jesus' teaching. As far as we know the first public words that came from the lips of Christ were, 'The time has come, the Kingdom of God is near' (Mark 1:15). He is clearly saying that that moment was the time of fulfilment of previous prophecies and proclamations and that something quite new was being commenced.

We read that Jesus preached from the beginning of His ministry to the end of His ministry about the Kingdom – 'from that time on' (Matt 4:17); that He went throughout Galilee and through all towns, villages and synagogues preaching the Kingdom of God (Matt 4:23, 9:35). In these passages, it seems that Matthew was at pains to point out how all encompassing this teaching of our Lord was, both in time and in place.

The Kingdom of God is a central topic in the Lord's prayer

(Matt 6). It is part of the first and last statements of the beatitudes (Matt 5:3,10) and the theme of half His parables. He sent out His disciples to preach a similar message (Matt 10:7), commanded His followers to seek first the Kingdom of God (Matt 6:33) and referred to it even during His trial (John 18:33-36).

In that crucial time of forty days between His resurrection and ascension, we read, 'He gave instructions through the Holy Spirit . . . and spoke about the Kingdom of God' (Acts 1:2-3). This period was 'prime time' for the Lord. If there was ever a time when He needed to emphasise the essentials of His teaching and ministry, it was during this period, to make sure that the disciples would fully appreciate the central point of His mission. No doubt the previous events of His death and resurrection would have given fresh insights to His followers as to the importance and relevance of this message about the Kingdom of God. Furthermore, the final things a person says prior to departing (or dying) are always very important and normally remembered.

It is interesting to note that Paul also spoke about the Kingdom of God at the end of his life, Acts 28:30. Further, if the Kingdom of God was not to be established until much later, why did Jesus spend such a lot of precious time talking about an event that would not affect the lives of His disciples? Surely this passage shows us very clearly that the Lord was preparing His followers for the immediate future not the distant future.

It is clear from the reading of the early verses of Acts 1 that the disciples were at least starting to appreciate the importance of the Kingdom message, if not its full implications. They asked Him if He was going to restore the Kingdom to Israel at that time (v6). Alas their vision was still limited, even though they had the best teacher in the world who was directed by the Holy Spirit (v2). There is some consolation here for those who seek to teach the truth of God and find people unable to fully grasp that truth! The disciples still saw the Kingdom in human terms and longed for the restoration of the nation of Israel, and, no doubt, the overthrow of the Roman Empire.

The answer of Jesus to the disciples' question of restoring

the Kingdom to Israel is interesting. He clearly indicates Israel has a significant future by His words, 'It is not for you to know times or dates that the Father has set' (v7) and then goes on to say that they will receive power when the Holy Spirit comes on them (v8). The context of this verse is very important. So often it has been emphasised that the descent of the Spirit at Pentecost saw the formation of the church, the release of spiritual gifts, produced the mighty preaching of Peter which resulted in many coming to faith in Christ. However we have often missed the fact that this verse was spoken in the context of teaching about the Kingdom of God. Putting it another way, when Jesus answered this question regarding the Kingdom and Israel in effect He said, "No, I'm not going to restore the Kingdom to Israel – that's not the point of what I am saying – But you are going to receive power and you are to witness to this Kingdom."

In summary, Jesus' ministry was one of both demonstration and extension of the Kingdom of God. When John the Baptist sent a message to Jesus inquiring as to whether or not He was the one who was to come from God, Jesus told them to tell John, 'The blind receive their sight, the lame walk, those who have leprosy are cured, the deaf hear, the dead are raised (extension and demonstration) and the good news is preached to the poor' (Luke 7:22).

Obviously John was having some questions about Christ. It is easy to imagine what was going through his mind as he sat in the prison cell. Was Jesus really the Messiah? What about the message that he (John) had been preaching about the Kingdom of God? Or, for that matter, this same message preached by Jesus Himself? If the Kingdom of God was present, why was he in prison? The Kingdom had come, but it was not here yet with irresistible power. Jesus said people were not to be offended (scandalised) at this paradox (Luke 7:23).

E. Stanley Jones commenting on the importance of the Kingdom message of Jesus says, 'It was the centre and the circumference of all He taught and did . . . The Kingdom of God is the master-conception, the master-plan, the master-purpose, the master-will that gathers everything up into itself and gives it redemption, coherence, purpose, goal.' (E. Stanley

Jones, Is the Kingdom of God realism? New York: Abingdon-Cokesbury, 1940, Pg 53).

The Kingdom – here, but not fully

There appear to be two parallel concepts about the Kingdom of God in the New Testament and these two concepts have been misunderstood and thus caused a considerable degree of confusion down through the ages. One concept is that the Kingdom of God is here at this present age and the other is that it will not appear until Christ returns. Verses supporting each of these positions can be found and much argument has occurred between proponents of each view.

It is probably true to say that the most widely held view today, is that the Kingdom of God has invaded this present age but has not totally replaced it. God's Kingdom will not be fully present until Jesus returns. This view seeks to synthesise aspects of both of the present and future views.

It is summarised by such statements as –

'We are living in the presence of the future'
'We experience a degree of realised eschatology'
'The future has invaded the present'
'The Kingdom of God is here but not fully'
'Already but not yet.'

This present/future dimension of the Kingdom of God is mirrored in other Biblical truth. For example in redemption, salvation and eternal life; we were redeemed (1 Pet 1:18) we will be redeemed (Rom 8:32), we are being saved (1 Cor 1:18) we will be saved (Rom 5:9), we now have eternal life,(1 Jn 3:14,Jn 17:3) we will have eternal life (Rom 6:22). Similarly we can say that the Kingdom of God is here (Lk 17:20-21, Matt 6:33, 21:31, 23:13, 12:25-28, 13:24ff, 37-42, Mk 1:15, Lk 16:16, Matt 16:28, Lk 22:29) and yet the Kingdom of God is still to come (Matt 25:31-34, Lk 13:22-30, 22:16,21:31, 19:11, 13:24-30).

The Kingdom – a present tension

The fact that the Kingdom of God is not yet fully realised means that as Christians we have to learn to live with an inevitable tension. This tension is between sin, the distortions and imperfections of the present, and the completeness and perfection of the future (1 Cor 13:8-12). Paul in Romans 8:18-

24 captures this tension very graphically where he says that, 'The whole of creation has been groaning . . . right up to this present time.' However we do have hope and it is this that saves us.

Margaret had cancer. It had been confirmed the lumps were malignant.

Over the next months we were to marshal our forces as a congregation to pray for her healing. The elders annointed her with oil and prayed for her. The congregation had times of prayer and fasting for her. Friends prayed, her home group prayed, she and her husband prayed, but Margaret died.

Why Lord?

Didn't we pray enough? Wasn't our faith great enough? How much do you need? Were you displeased with us? Question after question after question.

I still don't know. But perhaps Rom 8:18-21 gives us some insights. 'The creation is waiting in eager expectation for the sons of God to be revealed . . . The creation has been subjected to frustration . . . The creation itself will be liberated from its bondage to decay . . . The whole of creation is groaning.' Currently God's Kingdom is not fully upon us. When it comes fully, death, disease and sin will all be banished. We are part of a frustrated creation which is groaning and subject to decay. We must learn to live with incompleteness and imperfection. This is the hope of the gospel. I know of nobody who sees people healed everytime they pray for healing. I know of no congregation which has a 100% success rate in this area. We will all eventually die, unless the Lord returns before that event.

Something of this tension or incompleteness is also seen in the ministry of Jesus while here on earth. He was the Lord of Heaven but He did not overwhelmingly convince people that He was the Messiah. Neither was there such a demonstration of the Kingdom of God that everybody was convinced as to who He was or the validity of what He was teaching. Many people didn't respond to Him. He was misunderstood, finally rejected and deserted even by His own disciples. When people asked for spectacular proof in the form of signs, He refused to give it. However, too much was happening to ignore Him completely.

Similarly with the current ministry of the Holy Spirit. The Holy Spirit is only the first fruits (Rom 8:23), He is not the full harvest. He is the deposit (2 Cor 1:22), guaranteeing what is to come. His ministry is not automatically convincing, He can be resisted, grieved and ignored. There is yet to be a fuller revelation of the ministry of the Spirit, and for now, suffering is a part of the Kingdom and the Holy Spirit is the comforter.

As with the earthly ministry of Jesus and with the current ministry of the Holy Spirit, so with the current expression of the Kingdom of God. The Kingdom can be resisted (parable of the sower and seed, Matt 13:1-22). It will not destroy all evil (parable of wheat and tares, Matt 13:24-30). It is apparently insignificant – but growing (parables of yeast and mustard seed, Matt 13:31-33). Enough is happening to attract our attention and substantiate the presence of the Kingdom among us but failure reminds us that we do not have it all yet. There is a time coming when the Kingdom of God will be irresistible. Then, every knee will bow to Christ, the current tension will be relieved and sickness, death and tears will flee away and the ministry of the Spirit will be fully expressed. Until that time we live by faith, struggle with unanswerable questions and experience degrees of frustration.

This current age of the Kingdom of God is the age of grace. People have the right to accept or reject grace. It is the coming age which embraces the element of judgment, where the power and authority of the Kingdom of God will be displayed against those who have wilfully rebelled and rejected the grace of God. Then there will be no opportunity to choose. Jesus stopped short of proclaiming this in His reference to the Isaiah prophecy (Is 61:1-2) when He read from this passage in the synagogue at Nazareth (Lk 4:18-19). He had not come to inaugurate this aspect of God's Kingdom at that time. Holding the present and future dimensions of the Kingdom of God in appropriate balance prevents us from taking extreme views. To take the view that the Kingdom is only in the future, as dispensationalists do, leads to a pessimistic world view where the best thing Christians can do is man life boats and save souls. Such a view states that it is of no value whatsoever to rearrange the furniture while the ship is sinking.

I read recently in a local newspaper of a person holding

this position. Each week a reporter goes into the community and asks a cross-section of people the same question. The question, the people's answers and their photographs are then published in the paper. On this particular week the question was,

'Are you worried about the greenhouse effect and are you doing anything to protect the ozone layer?'

A response from a retired local man was, 'I believe the Lord will come soon before the greenhouse effect is noticed. I won't be replacing the CFC's (chlorofluorocarbons) I've got.'

His view of end time events was affecting the way he lived here and now. Such a view can lead Christians to a careless attitude about this world and our environment. A person holding a Kingdom view would probably answer the question about the greenhouse effect by saying, 'Yes, I am very concerned about the environment and the ozone layer. I am seeking to limit my use of CFC's. This world is God's and He expects us all to respect it and look after it for future generations.'

On the other hand, to accept the view that the Kingdom of God is fully here now, or will come fully before the return of Christ, is not facing reality. Neither the Kingdom of God nor the ministry of the Holy Spirit are at our beck and call. We are at theirs! God doesn't heal all sickness. We struggle with the debilitation of the aging process and we must still face death. None of these are expressions of the Kingdom of God. How many of us, who have been touched by renewal, struggle theologically after praying long and earnestly for healing for a Christian friend, just to see them die? Surely the reason that we do not see healing in all those who are prayed for, is due to the fact that the Kingdom of God is not yet here fully. When we are privileged to see sovereign and supernatural works of God we are witnessing an in-breaking of that Kingdom into the affairs of people.

God is pleased to show the power of His Kingdom in two main ways.

Causative power. Here His power operates to radically alter circumstances. An example of this is in Daniel 3 where Shadrach, Meshach and Abednego were placed in the fiery furnace and they came out without being singed, scorched or even any smell of fire on them. However those who threw them in were killed by the intense heat. God's power caused the normal effects of fire on the three men to be removed. Not only was God's power in evidence but He also received glory in this situation. A heathen king praised the God of Heaven.

Preservative power. Here God's power enables people to go through the circumstances. An example of this is the stoning of Stephen (Acts 7). In this situation God did not remove the effects of the circumstances (stoning) but gave Stephen the power to go through these circumstances. As he was being stoned he asked for forgiveness for his persecutors. Again we see that God was glorified in this event also. 'They laid their clothes at the feet of Saul' No doubt this event in Saul's life planted seeds which were to later bear fruit for the Kingdom of God.

God's causative power and preservative power both result in the same thing – glory to His name. In one case by removing the circumstances and in the other by taking people through the circumstances. We need to recognise that God still works this way today. The Joni Ereckson Tadas of this life bear just as effective a witness to the power of God as do the miraculous healings that we read of. In fact their testimony is often greater because it is an ongoing testimony.

Further, in these two illustrations God's power is linked to human faith. Shadrach, Meshach and Abednego trusted God implicitly. As Nebuchadnezzer threatened to throw them into the fire they said, 'God is able to deliver us and if he doesn't, we still won't bow down and worship your image' (Dan 3:17-18). What faith! Not presumptuous, not pessimistic. As Stephen was being stoned he was able to look up into heaven and say, 'Lord, do not hold this sin against them' (Acts 7:60). Such was his faith in God.

Faith in God whether He removes the circumstances or permits them to remain. Such faith enables God to demonstrate His Kingdom power and glorify His name in His people.

There is a bigger audience than just other human beings watching the events in the lives of Christians. The book of Job indicates that spiritual powers are also observing what is happening (Job 1:6-11). We do not understand the effect on

Satan's kingdom of Christians standing firm against the powers of darkness. Patient endurance in the face of opposition from the kingdom of darkness can be just as much a sign of the Kingdom of God as a miraculous event.

In this present age of tension between the 'already' and the 'not yet,' God can and will turn evil into good (Gen 50:19). We must be prepared to accept the power of God in which ever way He desires to manifest it. In doing so we will be vessels for His glory.

Lesslie Newbiggin has captured this present/future tension of the Kingdom of God very beautifully when speaking about the Kingdom of God. He says, 'It is not the lantern which the traveller in the dark carries in his hand; it is the glow on his face which reflects the coming dawn.' (Your Kingdom Come, Lesslie Newbiggin, John Paul Press, 1980, Pg 23)

This current tension keeps us from the two extremes of pessimism and triumphalism and it offers us a partial answer to many of the questions we struggle with. On the one hand, we must expect evidences of the inbreaking of the Kingdom of God among us and reach out in faith to embrace the possibility of such events; while on the other we can not demand such evidences. God is sovereign and we depend upon His grace and mercy. We have only tasted of the powers to come (Heb 6:5). There is much more to come yet. On this side of eternity our efforts will always be limited, partial and inadequate.

The Kingdom - our priority

The statement by Jesus to 'seek first the Kingdom of God and His righteousness' must stand out as a beacon in our Lord's teaching. The two concepts of 'earnestly striving after, with the highest priority' are contained in the words 'seek first' and in no other place in Scripture are these two words put together. What are we preoccupied with? What are our loyalties? Where do our motives stem from? What is the framework of reference for our congregations, our organisations or our communities? For Christians, all such questions must be answered in the context of this important commandment of our Lord. The human heart will never be fully satisfied if it settles for anything less than the Kingdom of God. Human beings were made to live within its boundaries. The Kingdom of God does not threaten men and women; it only threatens Satan and his kingdom. Men and women find their fullest potential within this framework.

This priority of the Kingdom of God has implications for us from the moment of conversion. The Bible has no such concept as Jesus being first our Saviour and then our Lord. In the New Testament Jesus is referred to as Saviour 16 times and as Lord 420 times. A deeper understanding of the Kingdom of God would have prevented this dichotomy between Jesus being Saviour first and Lord later, which has been widely accepted within the evangelical wing of the Church.

Lordship demands repentance. We were having a baptism at a beach one Sunday afternoon. It was a beautiful day and there were about 300 people gathered on the foreshore watching as people were being baptised. We had planned to baptise 5 people but finished up baptising 13. People came out of the crowd to obey the Lord or place their faith in God and be baptised there and then.

Frank had been watching the events. In fact he had been watching these Christians for quite a while. Other members of his family had come to the Lord and he had noticed the changes this had made. Frank is a Maori and he is a big guy. He had come from a small country town to work in the city. In the past he had been a violent man.

Finally on that Sunday afternoon God got him! From the back of the crowd gathered by the beach he made his way forward and crashed on his knees in the sand in front of everybody his whole body wracked with sobs as he repented his way back to God. From that time on things have been different. Often hard? Yes! But he has sought to live as a member of the Kingdom of God in his position as a leading hand on a building site. Frank has been involved with young people from off the streets, ministering to them with the love of Jesus. God has replaced his violence with a gentleness and love for young people. Frank has stuck to the Lord through thick and thin.

Jesus said, 'Repent, for the Kingdom of God is near' (Matt 3:2). Mere belief is not the way to enter the Kingdom. Deep heart-felt repentance is a prerequisite for successful participation in the Kingdom of God. We saw that in the life of Frank on the beach as he truly made Jesus Lord of his life that day.

An underpinning and appreciation of the Kingdom of God might also have helped prevent some of the many ruptures and schisms that have fractured and splintered so much of Protestantism. The issue must never be – What is our tradition? Or – What does our denomination say or believe? If we are to be faithful to the Matt 6:33 statement of Jesus it must be – 'What is the way of the Kingdom of God?' What a liberating theme the Kingdom of God is! Many of our personal struggles and those of our congregations can be traced to the fact that we have not understood or entered into the full implications of the Matthew 6:33 statement about the Kingdom of God.

The Kingdom – and the King

In any discussion on the Kingdom of God fears may be expressed that we are discussing the Kingdom and ignoring the King. It is certainly possible to emphasise the Kingdom at the expense of the King.

Over the centuries the Church of Jesus Christ has faced many controversies. Arguments have arisen over doctrinal issues, methods of outreach, matters of church structure and government. Inevitably people are forced to take sides on these issues and this causes tensions and hostility between opposing factions. I am sure that the devil loves this. He sidetracks Christians into fighting each other rather than fighting him. It's called divide and conquer!

In some of these issues the truth embraces both positions while in others it may lie between the two extremes of the argument.

Take for example the issue of the humanity and deity of Christ. Taking certain portions of the Scriptural record about Christ, good arguments can be made for each of these positions. We must therefore accept that Christ was at the same time both divine and human. To hold one at the expense of the other is error.

While there is no doubt that the emphasis of the teaching

of Jesus was focused on the Kingdom of God, neither is there any doubt about the emphasis of the Apostles teaching. They preached Christ crucified and risen. Numerous portions in Acts and the Epistles indicate this and of course the person of Christ and His work of salvation is absolutely central and an integral part of our faith.

Does this mean that we ignore the message that Jesus brought about the Kingdom of God by saying that the Apostles have up dated this and made what He said unimportant today? Surely not. Any attempt to make the Apostles' message more important than our Lord's or to separate the Gospels from Acts and the Epistles is a form of dispensationalism. Is this not a case of holding both rather than arguing for the priority of one over against the other?

We must recognise both the King and His Kingdom. There is no Kingdom if there is no King. Likewise the King came to establish His Kingdom. Jesus is the King, the Kingdom is His agenda. The Kingdom directs us to the King. The King leads us into the Kingdom. Here we have a dynamic interaction, there should be no dichotomy.

It was absolutely essential that in the early days of the Christian faith the Apostles preached about Christ. If they had only preached the Kingdom of God there would have been no gospel. Jesus was the face of the Kingdom. The reign of God had drawn near in Jesus and they had personally seen Him. The death and subsequent resurrection of Jesus had to be proclaimed, it was the final authentication of all that Christ had taught and done. Now the agenda of Jesus had been passed onto His followers. His resurrection made it possible for His followers to live in the reality of the Kingdom of God here and now.

So it is today – to preach the Kingdom of God without the King reduces Christianity to a programme or an ideology. Jesus must be central. Divorcing the person of Christ from the message of the Kingdom of God is like preaching about the Church and ignoring the Head, desiring the gifts without the Giver or healing without the Healer. We must seek the King and His Kingdom; recognise the Church and the Head; desire the gifts and the Giver; accept healing and the Healer.

On the other hand neither must we offer the King without

the Kingdom – this has often lead to privatised Christianity much of which has retreated into the bunker to wait for the return of Christ. The Kingdom is primarily the reign of God, or the Lordship of Jesus. Christians are to bring all they have and do under this reign.

It is quite legitimate to teach about aspects of the Church without teaching about the Head of the Church. On the other hand it is obviously wrong to continually discuss the Church ignoring the Head. Similarly with the Holy Spirit and His gifts (part of His agenda). So in teaching about the Kingdom of God, we must speak of Christ and His agenda. To ignore either is to be in error.

The last verse in Acts illustrates this point perfectly where we read that Paul 'preached the Kingdom of God and taught about the Lord Jesus Christ.'

A recent publication of the Kingdom Manifesto (see Appendix 1), put together by some evangelicals in this country, is an attempt to articulate some of the issues which result from the life, death and resurrection of the Lord. Issues that Christians need to address.

Some may ask, 'Why then use Kingdom terminology?'
We reply, 'Jesus did!'
Paul said 'that in all things he (Christ) might have the preeminence' (Col 1:18). Jesus said, 'Seek first the Kingdom of God and his righteousness' (Matt 6:33).
We must keep Christ and His Kingdom central in all that we do and say.
We can do both!
We must do both!

The Kingdom – a conclusion

In summary we see that the Kingdom is on the heart of Father. It was the main theme of the ministry of Jesus. It is the reason the Holy Spirit was given. It must therefore be central in all we do and think.

As we seek to understand the importance of this message, we must never forget that ultimately it is not a case of us getting hold of the Kingdom of God, but rather that the Kingdom of God must get hold of us!!

CHAPTER
NINE

EVIDENCE OF THE KINGDOM OF GOD

A young mother, Sue, was attending a pre-school with her child. She got talking to another mother who had just recently moved into the area and discovered that she was having a major problem with an eighteen month old baby who couldn't seem to get to sleep in a particular room in their new house. The baby would scream and scream when put down into its cot. Sue was immediately alerted to the fact that this may be due to some previous occult activity in that room and proceeded to explain this to the mother. The mother listened attentively but had very little understanding about such matters. However Sue left her with the invitation to contact her again if she could be of any help. Some days later the woman rang, she was desperate. Sue arranged for two men from the congregation to visit the home. When they arrived they discovered that the couple knew almost nothing about the Bible or Christ, so they took time to explain that they came in the authority of Jesus Christ, read a few verses from the Bible, and then prayed in each room of the house, seeking to bring the authority and peace of God into the home. That night when the baby was put down it slept peacefully right through the night and to my knowledge this problem has never occurred again. How did this affect the couple whose baby it was? They wanted to get a copy of that book the two men had read from!

This is a clear example of a non-Christian couple experiencing something of the power of the Kingdom of God. That may not not have brought them to faith in Christ but it did plant a seed of the Kingdom in their minds. We know that seeds have a habit of growing when the conditions are right. Jesus said, 'If I drive out demons by the Spirit of God then the

Kingdom of God has come upon you.' Matt 12:28.

Over the years we have been privileged to gain many insights into the Kingdom of God by observing some of the things that He has done in the lives of those in our fellowship. It seems that God has ordained that we can not learn the principles of His Kingdom by academic means only. We need to launch out in practice and faith with what we have and know before He will teach us more. We don't learn to swim by listening to someone talk about it in a classroom, we need to get in the pool and do it! So it is in the Kingdom of God. Jesus said, 'The measure you use, it will be measured to you – and even more. Whoever has will be given more; whoever does not have, even what he has will be taken from him' (Mark 4:24-25). Notice we have to use first and then we will get more.

Come with me as we learn together from the following examples. In some cases names have been changed to protect people's identity.

Through healing

Peter had had persistent coughs through the winter months and it was suggested that he should receive prayer for this. Earlier in his life, as a result of an accident, he had had his total spleen removed.

At a John Wimber seminar during a time of ministry there was a call for those who had disfunctional organs to receive prayer. Peter believed that this was the moment he should trust the Lord. As people gathered around him and started to pray for him he sensed pressure in the area where his spleen had been.

Returning home he believed that God may have done something quite remarkable in terms of his spleen and so arranged for an ultra-sound scan to be taken. When this was checked a round clear portion on the plate was seen. The explanation given by a radiologist was that to the best of his knowledge it was a fully formed spleen. The following winter Peter was free from the persistent coughs that had plagued him for so long.

We read that Jesus 'appointed seventy and sent them out two by two' and told them to "heal the sick who are there and tell them the Kingdom of God is near you"' (Luke 10:1-2,8-9). We were to discover that part of the message of the Kingdom of God was His authority over sickness and disease.

Through a child

A couple in the congregation had just discovered that the wife was pregnant for the third time. Both the previous pregnancies had seen the wife experiencing severe morning sickness which resulted in her spending much of the day in bed, thus causing a great deal of pressure to be placed on the household and marriage. True to form within a few weeks of this third pregnancy the wife was in bed much to the distress of the family. Their oldest child, a three year old daughter came into her mother's room one day. Standing at the door with her hands on her hips she said 'Mummy are you still sick? I am going to pray that Jesus will heal you.' With that she marched across the room to her mother's bed, placed her little hand on her mother's head and prayed a simple child's prayer that God would heal her mother. Later that day her mother was up, out of bed, and suffered no more morning sickness for the rest of her pregnancy.

Jesus said, 'Let the little children come unto me for of such is the Kingdom of God' (Matt 19:14). How simple are Kingdom principles for children. How complex for adults!

Away from God

I'm thinking of a young man of great potential. He once ran well for the Lord but now seems to be far away from Him.

Jesus said, 'No one who puts his hand to the plough and looks back is fit for the Kingdom of God' (Luke 9:62). What does this verse mean in terms of this young man's life? I don't know but I aim to encourage people who have started to serve the Lord and walk in the ways of His Kingdom to keep on going. Quitting is a serious matter.

Its cost

A man stood in front the principal of one of the major educational institutions in the country. He had come to tell his principal that he was going to resign as God had called him into full-time Christian service. (You understand of course that there is no such special category as full-time service when a person is in the Kingdom of God. Everybody is in full-time service for God in His Kingdom.)

The principal was dumbfounded. The man who stood in front of him had been one of the youngest people ever appointed to the position he had held. During the three years of his leadership of the department he had overseen, it had grown to be the one most sought-after by students.

'You're a fool' growled the principal. 'You could have been Director General of Education.'

The principal wasn't a prophet and it is most unlikely that what he said would ever have come true but Jesus said, "The Kingdom of Heaven is like a treasure hidden in a field. When a man found it, he hid it again, and then in his joy went and sold all he had and bought that field." (Matt 13:44). We were to discover that when a person glimpses the Kingdom, it unleashes a powerful motivation to serve the King. Billy Graham was once asked if he would run for President of the USA. When refusing to consider this he was asked if the job was too big for him. He is reputed to have said 'No, the job was too small, God has called me to something much bigger.'

In Mission

It was reported during the Russian army's occupation of Afghanistan that Russian Christians were being conscripted into the Russian army because of their faith in Christ. They were then sent to the war in Afghanistan. While in Afghanistan they witnessed to Afghan Moslems and saw them come to faith in Christ. Now if that is not a turn around what is? Russian Christians, punished for faith in Christ, leading Moslems to that same faith in a country closed to missionary influence. Sometimes the devil seems to overstep himself.

Jesus said, 'The gospel of the Kingdom of Heaven will be preached in the whole world as a testimony to all nations and then the end will come.' God has His own ways of penetrating impregnable barriers with the message of His Kingdom.

Provision of resources

A ministry had commenced among street kids and the

couple running it had about 16 living with them in a small three bedroomed home. It was obvious that further accommodation would be needed but where could it be found. Ideally a property with some land would be the best.

One Saturday the husband was looking through the newspaper at properties to lease and saw a 50 acre farm available, not far out of the city. A number of people looked it over. The property was signed up and the couple with their extended family moved in. Further accommodation was built and the work developed rapidly.

About eight months after they moved onto the farm, the neighbour two along and to the left of the 50 acre farm approached the husband with an offer to lease him a piggery and sell him the 120 breeding sows. With the lease went a small house ideal for a full-time couple working with the expanding ministry. Money was forthcoming and the piggery and further house were leased.

About three months later the neighbour between the 50 acre property and the piggery notified the couple that his property would be available, rent free. It had a house and four acres of land. All he required was that the land was put into vegetables and he received half the earnings.

To the right of the 50 acre farm was another house. This was being used for drug dealing and those in the ministry started to 'pray the dealers out'. You guessed it. Within a short period of time the owner of the drug dealers house removed the tenants and offered it to the ministry for a rental. Humanly speaking, what are the chances that four homes, adjacent to each other in a rural area, would become available in less than two years for use by those seeking to minister for the Lord? Probably nil.

Jesus speaking in the sermon on the Mount about possessions said 'seek first the Kingdom of God and his righteousness and all these things will be added unto you' (Matt 6:33). What were the 'these things?' Material possessions needed to get His work done. We learnt that when God finds people to do His work and they need material possessions with which to do it, then He is faithful to provide for those needs.

Serving in humility

A young man had been hassled at work by his fellow work mates for being a Christian. He was a mechanic and fairly new to the job. One weekend, to the shock of the whole workshop, one of the young mechanics was tragically killed in a car accident. The following week nobody wanted to clear out the dead man's locker except, that is, the young man who was the Christian.

Jesus said 'I tell you the truth, unless you change and become like little children, you will never enter the Kingdom of heaven. Therefore whoever humbles himself . . . is the greatest in the Kingdom of heaven' (Math 18:3-4).

The Kingdom of God is not established by the methods of this world, such as pressure tactics, by politics or the arrogant aggressive ways of ambitious men and women. The Kingdom of God is advanced by men and women in work places being prepared to humbly serve their fellows.

In finance

I sat across the room from an excited young couple who had called to see me after a day's work. The evening before the husband had phoned me and said that they wanted to come round and talk to me about Kingdom finance. Knowing that they were struggling financially I presumed they wanted to talk about budgeting. But when they arrived it was obvious that they had not come around to talk about financial difficulties, their faces told me that I was about to hear something else.

The story unfolded. Some months previously the wife had been praying and saying to the Lord that she would really like to be out of debt so that they could give more money to Him.

Two weeks ago, to their utter surprise, they had come into some money. As they been praying about how they should use it they sensed that God wanted them to give most of it away.

You can imagine my surprise when they said they wanted to give $300,000 to our congregation's community trust to be used for helping people get into their own accommodation. I urged them to go away and think more about this decision, but they were quite convinced that this was what God was wanting and they were so happy that they were able to do it.

Jesus said, 'The Kingdom of heaven is like a man who scatters seed on the ground. Night and day, whether he sleeps or gets up, the seed sprouts and grows though he does not know how. All by itself the soil produces grain, first the head then the stalk and then the kernel' (Mark 4:26-29).

About three years prior to the young couple approaching me with the offer of this money, we had been teaching the congregation about the resources of money and possessions which we as Christians had. We had sown the 'seed' of Kingdom finances and the possibility of Christians releasing more of what God had given them for use in His Kingdom. That seed had been growing in the minds of this young couple during those three preceeding years, it had produced the kernel.

Truth about the Kingdom of God is like that. It has a time fuse on it, then it explodes into life, often years after the fuse was initially lit.

God has been gracious to us. We have seen His hand in these and many other instances. Through such illustrations He has enlarged our understanding of His ways and sent shafts of light penetrating our understanding about His Kingdom rule. His Kingdom is far grander than we can ever appreciate with our limited capacity for spiritual truth. He wants our understanding to grow.

Jesus said that the knowledge of the secrets of the Kingdom of heaven have been given to His followers (Matt 13:11). Let's seek the Lord for further secrets together.

CHAPTER
TEN

CONFLICT OF THE KINGDOMS

A Christian friend of mine had been invited by a group of young people to come and watch as they played with a ouija board. Coming from a fairly conservative theological background he believed that such practices were hocus pocus. He strongly denied any possibility of spiritual power being able to affect the physical area of life and so he went along to see what all the excitement was about.

During the evening his cynicism was rudely shattered. The glass tumbler, which the young people were using on the board, inexplicably shattered during some of their so called hocus pocus! Both he, and those present, were terrified. He later confessed to being quite unprepared to deal with the distress of the young people that night.

In our ordered, rational, scientific, materialistic, Western world such an event often has no place. We tend to deny its reality or try to explain it away with plausible explanations.

The Bible however paints a very different picture. It acknowledges that there are very powerful spiritual forces at work on this planet, locked in a gigantic cosmic battle. In fact it presents two kingdoms. The Kingdom of God and the kingdom of Satan, which are the absolute antithesis of each other.

In Matthew 12:22-28 we read of Jesus healing a blind and mute man. When the religious leaders heard what had happened they attributed this healing to Beelzebub. Jesus 'knew their thoughts' and said, 'Every kingdom divided against itself will be ruined . . . If Satan drives out Satan, he is divided against himself. How then can his kingdom stand?' Jesus goes on to say, 'But if I drive out demons by the Spirit of God, then the Kingdom of God has come upon you.' Clearly

Satan has a kingdom and his kingdom is in opposition to that of God's.

The whole of human history can be examined from the point of view of the conflict between these two Kingdoms. An understanding of this conflict can give us keys and insights by which we can more effectively 'seek first the Kingdom of God.' It can help us in our Christian life and ministry, in our prayer life and service for God. It can give us a perspective of what is really happening in the world and enables us to interpret world events through different eyes.

The early chapters of Genesis show us that God created a marvellous universe. It is His handiwork and masterpiece. The creation is not the result of an infinite series of random or chance events. Beauty and order can not be created out of non-beauty and disorder in such a manner. When we look around and see the immensity and power of this creation, it is much harder to believe the other alternatives presented to account for the origin of the universe. The more we discover about this order and beauty of the universe, the more astonishing it appears.

God also created this planet. With the aid of high resolution colour photographs taken in space, we can now see just how beautiful it is. A shining blue orb, revealing brown land masses and speckled with white clouds suspended against an inky black background.

My sons and I enjoy scuba diving. Off our West coast is a cluster of islands, the Poor Knights, reputed to be among the top dozen diving spots in the world. Part of this area is a marine reserve and here something of the fauna of the tropics merges with the fauna and flora of the colder, southern oceans. The visibility is superb in all directions. On a fine day the sunlight filters down a hundred feet or so. It has been our privilege to dive here and view the magnificent shoals of fishes. You can view hundreds of small fish changing direction simultaneously as they dart away from larger predators or human intruders. How do they do that without bumping into each other? To view the incredible array of brightly coloured sponges and swim above a two metre Manta Ray, as it effortlessly glides through the water, is a breath-taking experience. The rocky shores plunge almost straight down and every available square millimetre is thickly encrusted with life of the most incredible variety. For those who have never dived it is impossible to describe this wonderworld of God's creation. The more we discover about this planet, the more marvellous it appears. The colour, the life, the variety, the intricacy, the splendour leave us in no doubt about the creative genius of the Maker.

However, the pinnacle of God's creation was the creating of men and women. They are God's masterpiece, His finest creative act and endeavour. Psalm 139:14 tells us that we are 'fearfully and wonderfully made.' From the order and control mechanisms seen within the individual cells, to the coordination of the glands and organs. From the amazing complexity and ability of the human brain, to the engineering of the skeleton and musculature, every human being bears witness to the creative ability of the maker. However, men and women are much more than biological machines, they are a unique part of God's creation for three reasons:

i. *Human beings are created in the image of God.*

There is no other part of God's creation that has this recorded about it. No sunset, or mountain or starry galaxy is made in God's image. Men and women alone, reflect something of the very nature and character of the Creator Himself. We are unique in that we inhabit both the physical and spiritual domain. Something that no other part of God's creation does.

ii. *Human beings are created to enjoy fellowship with God.*

This also sets them apart from the rest of God's creation. Animals, stars, planets, mountains, seas, plants, none of these parts of God's creation can have fellowship with God. Even angels don't seem to be able to fellowship with God in the same way that men and women can.

iii. *Human beings are created with a freedom to choose.*

Animals operate largely through instinct. The incredible division of responsibility in a beehive and its intricate workings are not the result of choice on behalf of the bees. Such co-operation has been pre-programmed by the creator to operate in this way. Of all of God's creation only human beings have the power of choice.

These three remarkable features set human beings apart from the rest of God's creation.

It is towards this masterpiece of God's creation, human beings, that Satan directed his attack.

The early chapters of Genesis tell us that Satan came to Adam and Eve with a temptation to disobey the clear command of God. Men and women succumbed and they yielded their allegiance to Satan, obeying him rather than God. Thus they came under his authority and rulership and became members of his kingdom. In fact, sin has affected the whole of God's creation. Romans 8:22 tells that the 'Whole of creation is groaning.' It is not just that human beings have been affected by sin, everything has. The whole of creation is like a coiled up spring, it's in tension, waiting for the full release of this planet and its people from the influences of sin. We read in 2 Corinthians 4:4 that 'Satan is the god of this world' and 1 John 5:19 tells that 'the world is under the control of the evil one.' During Jesus' temptation, Satan offered Him 'all the kingdoms of this world' (Luke 4:5). This temptation would have had no weight at all if these kingdoms were not Satan's to offer. Satan has the kingdoms of this world in his control.

What were these kingdoms which Satan offered Jesus? We are not told, but could they be the political, economic, educational kingdoms of men and women? Maybe they are social kingdoms, the racial kingdoms or even religious kingdoms. Any areas of society that are out of order, that do not demonstrate the ways of God – Satan holds these in his hands and seeks to exploit and control all of the activities of God's masterpiece. He is an evil genius who is skillfully manipulating the political, economic, educational, social, racial and religious systems of this world to his own ends and purposes. The Bible indicates that he is intelligent, that he is crafty and that he has spiritual beings and forces under his control that do his bidding.

Satan, however, does not own this world or the men and women who inhabit it. He is a usurper of what is rightfully God's. He is an alien and an illegal squatter on God's property. This does not mean that we can blame all human wickedness on Satan, thus absolving human beings from any responsibility in this matter. However, the origin and root of all evil is traced to Satan. We can liken the fall of Adam and Eve to the releasing of the brake of a driverless 10-tonne truck sitting at the top of a steep slope. When Adam and Eve disobeyed God, sin was unleashed on this planet. The sinfulness of human nature and the penetration of the world's systems by evil, means that much sinful activity now occurs without the direct influence of Satan and his forces and this seems to be gaining in momentum.

Furthermore the story of Job indicates that there is a certain limit placed on the Devil's activities. When Satan comes to God and challenges Him to remove His protection from Job, God places a limit on the extent to which Satan can go in his dealings with Job (Job chapters 1 & 2).

Sin and Satan have 'screwed up' the following areas of human life and endeavour:

i. *Human relationships.*

Relationships in marriages, families, and between races have all been affected as a result of Satan and sin. Sin has turned people into selfish, proud, competitive beings. Suspicion, fear and rejection often characterise our responses towards those who disagree with us or are different from us. We witness tensions between nations, tensions in politics, tensions between employee and employer, tensions in marriage and family. The first few chapters of Genesis illustrate this where we read of the first murder, a brother takes the life of a brother. Such difficulties in human relationships was not God's purpose for men and women, He never created them in this way. This is the effect of the kingdom of darkness in the lives of people.

ii. *Work and economics.*

Work was instituted before the fall. God intended Adam and Eve to work in the garden. In co-operation with Him, work was to be a creative, fulfilling, productive and rewarding enterprise. After sin entered God's creation, human beings' relationship to work changed. It became 'painful toil.' There would be opposition to people's endeavour – 'thorns and thistles.' After the fall it became HARD work – 'by the sweat of your brow' (Gen 3:17-19). Satan introduced something at the fall that caused people's relationship to work to change and that change has also affected the economics of this planet.

iii. Sexual areas.

Sexual relationships, something which God made sacred and ordained to be a creative act between a man and a woman, Satan has defiled and sin has twisted and spoiled. Pornography, homosexuality, premarital sex, extramarital sex, lesbianism, incest, bestiality and adultery – all of these words convey the spoiling effect of Satan's influence on the 'masterpiece' of God's creation. Satan has put his grubby fingers all over something which God made sacred.

iv. Men and women's innate desire to worship God.

That capacity and desire to worship, which God placed in men and women and meant it to be directed towards Himself, Satan has focused onto the occult and false religion. He has deflected it onto the worship of self, success, money and fame. This too has been twisted and distorted by Satan and sin.

v. Areas of the Church.

He has attacked the very fundamentals of Christian faith; the resurrection, the Scriptures, the virgin birth, the miracles of Christ. Humanism has infiltrated the Church replacing obedience to the Holy Spirit with trust and reliance on self. Sin has set Christian brother against Christian brother and sister against sister. Sin and Satan have caused division and conflict in the Body of Christ down through the ages.

There is no doubt that something has happened to the creation that God made. The kingdom of Satan has insidiously, ingeniously, and subtly impacted all of the affairs of men and women on this planet. We do not understand the full implications of this and it is probably good that we don't – it may be more than we could handle. When we view the news on our television screens we are viewing the effects of Satan's kingdom on this planet. It's not just people against people, Arabs against Jews in the Middle East, or Catholics against Protestants in Northern Ireland. It's a conflict of kingdoms.

Behind the distress on this planet there are spiritual powers manipulating, orchestrating and influencing all that we see. Ephesians 6:12 tells us that we 'wrestle against rulers . . . authorities, against the powers of this dark world and against the spiritual forces of evil in the heavenly realms.' With the best will in the world, political solutions will not be sufficient – at the best they will only be temporary. We don't deal with spiritual realities with human means. Spiritual power must be dealt with by spiritual power and this, of course, is the message of the gospel.

That's the bad news!

The good news is that Jesus came to this planet. This planet, dominated by sin and the kingdom of Satan, where Satan's rule and dominion was evident. This planet, Satan's home territory, usurped from God. Jesus came to this planet, enemy territory, in the form of a baby. Is there anything as weak and helpless as a human baby?

Now the full thrust of Satan's activity was turned against Jesus. He threw everything he had at Jesus. He used Herod, a political leader of the day, to make an edict that all baby boys should be killed. To save His life, His parents fled with Him into Egypt. Satan tempted Him in the wilderness and stirred up a demonic storm on the lake against Him. People tried to drive Him over the edge of a cliff. The devil's intention was to deflect Him from the purposes that the Father had for Him.

It is interesting to note that in the Old Testament there are very few references to Satan and his activities. However, in the New Testament there are many references to Satan and his demonic hordes. It's almost as if the coming of Jesus flushed out Satan and revealed the degree to which Satan's kingdom had influenced this planet. Light showed up darkness. Demons screamed in the presence of the Son of God.

Although the full force of Satan's attention was turned onto Jesus, Jesus lived a sinless life. He could say, 'The prince of this world has nothing in me' (John 14:10). Jesus did not succumb to the pressure of the prince of this world. There was nothing that Satan could put his finger on, there was no fear, no guilt and no greed in Jesus. He resisted all that Satan threw at Him. If this had not been the case, He would have been just like us and could not have been the Saviour.

Jesus went into death. Now death is not the domain of the Kingdom of God. Death is the result of sin and all sin traces its origin to Satan. Death is the innermost sanctum of the kingdom of Satan and Jesus voluntarily went into death and therefore came under the control of Satan. Let's try to illustrate. Imagine an old English castle. Moat, drawbridge, high walls, turrets. Under the castle is the dungeon – the castle's securest part. Heavy doors, locks, no way of escape. The castle represents Satan's stronghold, his kingdom. The dungeon represents death. Jesus comes to that castle and lives among its inhabitants. He allows Himself to be taken and placed in the dungeon. What did Satan think when he saw the Son of God hanging on the cross about to die? Hanging there in the darkness, deserted by His followers, experiencing all of the sinfulness and rebellion of humanity crushing down on His sinless soul, forsaken by His Father. Here the intimacy of Trinity was shattered! Surely this is where the conflict between the kingdoms reaches its climax.

Satan no doubt thought he was destroying the Son of God. Jesus told a parable which possibly gives us an insight into what was going on in the devil's mind at this moment. A man went into a foreign country and left some tenants in charge of his vineyard. When he sent his servants back to get some fruit from the vineyard, the tenants beat them and they returned to him empty handed. So he sent his son. 'They will respect him,' he said. But they killed him, thinking that by killing the heir the vineyard would be theirs (Matt 21:33-40). Was this the response of Satan as he saw Jesus dying on the cross? Did he think that by destroying the Son of God he would become the owner of this planet? We know that Jesus voluntarily went into death. He could say, 'No man takes my life from me. I lay it down of myself' (John 10:18). He was placing Himself into the innermost sanctum of Satan's kingdom.

We know the end of this event. Jesus rose from the dead. Death couldn't hold Him. He shattered its bands and so destroyed Satan's ace card. Thus the Christian message rests on the resurrection of Jesus. 'If Christ be not raised, your faith is in vain, you are yet in your sins' said the apostle Paul (1 Cor

15:14).

In Hebrews 2:14 we read – 'Since the children have flesh and blood, he too shared in their humanity so that by his death he might destroy him who holds the power of death – that is the devil – and free those who all their lives were held in slavery by their fear of death.'

Surely one of the most amazing statements in all of Scripture! Jesus came into enemy territory. He shared our humanity, taking on the weaknesses of a human body. As a human being, He entered the very arena where human beings were held captive. By going into death, the strongest part of Satan's kingdom, He destroyed him who holds the power of death – Satan. By doing so He brought about the possibility of release for all of God's creation.

Now that wasn't on Satan's agenda!

If he had really known what was happening, Satan would not have crucified the Lord of Glory. We read, 'If the princes of this world had understood . . . they would not have crucified him' (1 Cor 2:8).

To take on Satan at his strongest point and to destroy that point by becoming part of it, causes mere human beings to stand in awe and astonishment. There is an incredible mystery here, something that we can not fully understand or appreciate. If we had planned the defeat of Satan's kingdom we would have probably planned to smash it from without by superior power rather than from within by submitting to it.

There is no other religion on earth which has this concept at its heart. That the leader, makes Himself so vulnerable, as to voluntarily let Himself be taken into the opposition's securest territory.

At the cross, it appeared as if the kingdom of Satan had crushed the Kingdom of God. But God's foolishness and apparent weakness breaks through (1 Cor 1:18-2:5).

There is much more to the Christian message than just a man dying and rising again. The death and resurrection of Christ was a contest between opposing spiritual forces. It resulted in the destruction of a power which had held captive God's masterpiece for centuries. Satan's kingdom has been thoroughly disrupted. It has had its foundation cut from under it. His kingdom must now yield to the Kingdom of God in the followers of Jesus. His kingdom is now vulnerable, his authority undermined, his days are numbered. Hallelujah!

Jesus has been proclaimed as head over all things as Ephesians 1:18-23 so graphically says –

'I pray also that the eyes of your heart may be enlightened ... to know his incomparably great power for us who believe. That power is like the working of his mighty strength, which he exerted in Christ when he raised him from the dead and seated him at his right hand in the heavenly realms, far above all rule and authority, power and dominion, and every title that can be given, not only in the present age but also in the one to come. And God placed all things under his feet and appointed him to be head over everything for the church, which is his body, the fulness of him who fills everything in every way.' Christ is now Lord for the Church.

Jesus told Nicodemus that those who are born again become part of the Kingdom of God (John 3:3). To be in the Kingdom of God is to have been 'rescued from the dominion of darkness and brought into Kingdom of the Son he loves' (Col 1:13). This occurs through repentance from sin and faith in Jesus Christ as Lord and Saviour.

Lives that have been screwed up by sin and Satan can be restored to wholeness, usefulness and beauty and relationship with the maker.

Nancy had many unhappy memories of childhood and experienced much emotional abuse. She had been sexually molested by her father's friend at the age of ten. Had a breakdown at 16 and, at the age of 19, was viciously raped by two men. All of this had caused resentment and hatred to build up in her. She got involved in the drug scene and prostitution, had several lesbian relationships, was involved in crime and spent time in prison. She had two difficult marriages in which both husbands died.

Nancy had deep hurts and much bitterness in her life when she came to Christ. Instantly her life was changed and over a period of time she experienced deep emotional healing through the love and cleansing of Christ. She became involved with those who had come from similar backgrounds and saw God changing other people's lives as He had changed hers. In 1 Corinthians 6:9-11 we read, 'Do you not know that the wicked will not inherit the Kingdom of God? Do not be deceived neither sexually immoral nor idolaters nor adulterers nor male prostitutes nor homosexuals . . . will inherit the Kingdom of God. And that is what some of you were but you are washed, you are sanctified you are justified in the name of our Lord Jesus Christ and by the Spirit of God.'

We were to see the amazing transformation that can come into a person's life when it is washed, sanctified, justified and placed under the rule and reign of God.

Human beings were not created to live in the kingdom of darkness, they don't belong there. Our neighbours don't belong there. Our communities don't belong there. Our nations don't belong there. All were made for relationship with God, made in His image and created to live within His Kingdom.

Nor is the Kingdom of God a threat to human beings. Living within its jurisdiction people find their highest fulfilment. The Kingdom of God is only a threat to Satan and his kingdom.

However the battle is not yet over. The main victory is won, but there is still a mopping up exercise to be carried out. Conflict still rages between the two kingdoms. This has been so since the resurrection of Jesus. Men and women are in an arena, a war. This war has ebbed and flowed. Sometimes the Kingdom of God has been in the ascendancy, with great times of outpouring of the Holy Spirit and revivals.

In the Welsh revival, we are told that policemen were out of work and formed male quartets which sang in missions! At other times the Church has been in retreat. Countries have been closed to the gospel, or an apathetic Church has allowed the world to squeeze it into its mould. However it is God's intention to win back all the systems of this world that Satan has taken captive – God wants to 'reconcile all things to himself through Christ' (Col 1:19). The ultimate prize is the kingdoms of this world and in a coming day these will all be Christ's. Revelation 11:15 tells us of a day when 'the Kingdoms of the world have become the kingdom of our Lord and of his Christ, and he will reign for ever and ever.' The theme of the book of Revelation is the Kingdom. Reign, rule, kingdom, power, glory, honour, righteousness – are words which occur frequently.

Today we live in a day of grace. It is a time when God is patiently seeking to bring people to Himself through love and mercy. This age is not the age when God uses raw power to win the current conflict. That day is coming, when 'every knee will bow, in heaven and on earth and under the earth and every tongue confess that Jesus Christ is Lord' (Phil 2:10-11) and Satan will be cast from the presence of God forever. There is no doubt as to who has the greatest power. The death and resurrection of Jesus have demonstrated this for all time.

Scripture seems to indicate that we should expect a heating up of this conflict towards the end of this age. Paul tells Timothy that 'there will be terrible times in the last days' (2 Tim 3:1), and, 'in later times some will abandon the faith and follow deceiving spirits' (1 Tim 4:1). However the ultimate victory is assured. Jesus Christ is going to return in power and glory to this planet. I've taken a peep at the last chapter of the book!

We cannot fully understand our Christian faith unless we understand the conflict between these two kingdoms. Christianity is not just about a great man who gave wise teaching. It is not just a religious system with some very profound ideas about living. At the heart of our Christian faith is Christ. Christ living in the lives of His followers, seeking to counteract all the effects of sin and Satan within those lives and also within the communities in which His followers live.

CHAPTER
ELEVEN

MONEY, MATERIALISM
AND THE KINGDOM OF GOD

' "Good news to the poor," means that every person has a right to as much of the material things as will make them mentally, spiritually and physically fit for the purposes of the Kingdom of God, the rest belongs to the needs of others.' (E Stanley Jones. "The Unshakeable Kingdom and the Unchanging Person." Pg116. Abingdon Press.)

We were sitting together, a senior Zairean missionary friend and myself. We had been discussing some of the difficulties associated with that land and my friend had been explaining how so many of the Christians in Zaire were still locked into spiritism and witchcraft. He told me how elders of churches would visit the witchdoctor when they were sick. He spoke of pressure being placed on Christian families to seek help from such sources when members of their family were ill. He recounted an instance where at a communion service the presiding elder had prayer for the communion and then placed some special needles in the cup. These had literally jumped straight out again. This at the communion table! I was shocked.

In our congregation, involvement with the occult was always something we sought to deal with as soon as a person came to faith in Christ. I expressed my concern and wondered how people could be so 'blind' to these areas. He looked at me for a moment, and then, with great sadness, said something which I will never forget. 'Brian,' he said, 'spiritism in Zaire equals materialism in this country. They are both demonic. The majority of Christians here are just as blind to the effects of materialism on their Christian lives as Zairean Christians are to the effects of spiritism.'

I have thought a lot about that statement over the following years and I am quite sure that he had his finger right on the issue. I haven't heard of many Charismatics or Pentecostals seeking to cast out demons of greed or covetousness! I think there is a message there somewhere!

How many congregations never have difficulties with finance?

Why, with so many labour saving devices in the modern home are we still so busy?

Which church or Christian organisation has more money than they can use?

Why does society have the impression that the Church is always asking for money?

How is it that so many congregations suffer from a lack of committed people?

How much more could be achieved for the Kingdom of God if there was a greater release of finance and possessions?

The answer to all these questions revolves around Christians' attitudes towards and uses of their money and possessions. Our lives are inextricably intertwined with the gaining and use of money and material possessions. We spend many thousands of hours of our lives earning money and many more hours getting, using and maintaining our possessions. We think about ways of saving money and dream about things we would like to have, activities we would like to engage in and places we would like to visit. It would be a sobering exercise for each of us to sit down and try to calculate just how much time each week we spend in the pursuit and use of money and material possessions.

Because of the all-embracing nature of money and material possessions, we can not avoid it when we consider the topic of the Kingdom of God.

If the over-arching theme of Christ's message was the Kingdom of God, then I believe the single most important topic within that theme is our use of money and possessions. Any attempt to live within the principles of God's Kingdom will bring us face to face with this topic and will shine a spotlight on our attitudes towards money and possessions.

Topics such as justice and the poor, themselves crucial Kingdom topics, normally find their practical expression in the use and abuse of material possessions and money.

For many Western Christians, this topic may cause us to be uncomfortable. Then, shouldn't the gospel always challenge our comfort levels!! The subject creates considerable embarrassment. People become defensive and if someone suggests that we should leading more disciplined lives in this area, we are quick to justify ourselves, our lifestyles and our spending habits.

During the past 25 years, we have seen an astonishing frankness and openness develop in talking about many of our own needs. People have been prepared to talk more openly to others about personal weaknesses, marriage needs and even sexual problems. Is the area of the use of my money and possessions the last bastion against frankness? Most pastors, including this one, are locked into a materialistic system. We find it very difficult to speak openly on this matter. To do so, may even be a threat to a pastor's position. In our congregation, as in congregations of most Western countries, we have a long way to go in gaining a deeper appreciation of the implications of this topic.

Yet if there is an area which is tearing the heart and soul out of Western Christianity, it must be this one. The topic absorbs our time and energy. It places pressures on families to keep up with the lifestyle of those around. The acquisition of material possessions and the comforts of life make us soft and undisciplined and much of our current spiritual malaise in the West is a direct result of our affluence. Material goods have become a substitute for faith and as John White so accurately points out, 'Enslavement to the visible makes faith in the invisible suspect.'

An incredible resource

If the pitfalls associated with money and possessions are great, then so also is their potential in the Kingdom of God. Jesus told a parable about a shrewd manager (Luke 16:1-15). It is a parable that many of us have seldom considered and have probably never heard a sermon about it, but it is a parable of profound importance in this day and age. The parable goes like this. A rich man's manager was asked to give account of his master's finances. The manager called in two debtors, asked them how much they owed the rich man, then told them they could finalise the bill by paying a reduced amount. The rich man approved of the manager's dealings and said he was shrewd in the way he had handled this matter. Jesus uses this illustration to make some important observations.

In verse 8 Jesus says, 'The people of this world are more shrewd in dealing with their own kind than are the people of the light.' In other words, the ways non-christians use their money to further their causes are more shrewd than the ways Christians use their money for the furtherance of the Kingdom of God. What He is saying is that 'people of the light' have yet to discover the enormous resource that God has given them to use for His ways.

In verse 9 'worldly wealth' (NIV), is the translation from the Greek which is 'unrighteous mammon.' Here we see something even more profound. Something unrighteous can be used to honour God. How is money unrighteous?

Money is often used for immoral or illegal purposes. As the love of money is the root of all evil, we may be the recipient of money that has been gained illegally or immorally somewhere along its use. How many times does money pass through our hands which has been used to bribe another person, or was acquired as a result of exorbitant charges, unethical dealings, was stolen, or exchanged hands as a result of such activities as prostitution? We can never tell, but somewhere in its use the money we receive may have been acquired through unrighteous purposes. We become part of a chain of events in the use of that money. By receiving money from a person who has gained it through immoral or illegal means we are, in a way, perpetuating that immoral or illegal event. In a sense we support that action by permitting that person to pay a debt they owe us, with credit gained by unsavory means from another. Of course we do it unwittingly and can not be held in any way responsible for that person's action.

Verse 9 Jesus goes on to say that we should 'use worldly wealth to gain friends for yourselves so that when it is gone, you will be welcomed into eternal dwellings.' Here He is saying that we can turn money to our advantage. It will gain friends here and when we have finished with this life, these friends will welcome us into heaven. Why will they welcome us thus? Because we have used our resources to bring them to faith in Christ. What an incredible use of unrighteous mammon! What a potential it contains!

Verses 10 and 11 explain, 'Whoever can be trusted with very little can be trusted with much, and whoever is dishonest with very little will be dishonest with much. So if you have not been trustworthy in handling worldly wealth, who will trust you with true riches?' Jesus is explaining that, contrary to the way we feel so often about money, it is only a little thing. If we can't be trusted with this little thing, who will trust us with true riches. In this passage He doesn't explain what true riches are, but on the basis of other scriptures, we assume that they have to do with things other than material possessions. Authority and responsibility in His Kingdom perhaps? Our handling of money is a yardstick by which God measures our trustworthiness.

Verse 13 tells us, 'No servant can serve two masters. Either he will hate the one and love the other, or he will be devoted to the one and despise the other. You cannot serve both God and Money.' This is a disturbing statement. It places money in direct competition with our allegiance to God. Devoted to one, despising the other. Hating one, loving the other!

How do we serve money? Is it by being preoccupied with it and seeking to get as much as we can? Is it the financiers of this world, or the super-rich that are the money servers? This may be true. But we cannot deflect this question from ourselves this easily. We all serve money when we let it make decisions for us. For example, I need to buy a new car, not something I am very fond of doing I should add.

What is my first consideration?

Normally it is, 'What can I afford?'

Who then is making this decision, myself or money?

Suppose I can afford a $20,000 car, does this make it right to spend that much? Perhaps God would have me buy a $6,000 car and give the rest to Him. Or maybe I believe it is in God's purposes for me to get a $10,000 car and I can only afford $7,000. What about trusting God for the balance? The question, 'Whom do we serve,' can be rephrased, 'Who makes decisions for us?' I suggest that we all serve money much more than we are aware of. When we serve money we are not serving God!

Verse 14 describes the religious leaders' response to Jesus' teaching. 'The Pharisees, who loved money . . . sneered.' Lovers of money are mentioned several times in the New Testament. Elders of the congregation are to be people who do not love money (1 Tim 3:3, 1 Pet 5:2). I wonder how often this test is applied before the selection of leadership? We read that in the last days people would be especially characterised by their love of money (2 Tim 3:2). Christians are urged to keep themselves free from the love of money (Heb 13:5) and we are told that the love of money is the root of all kinds of evil (1 Tim 6:10).

Money has an enormously powerful hold on society and individuals. In fact it is possibly the most powerful of a triad of addictive forces that affect people, these being – sex, power (over others, such as political, military, physical, economic) and money. Money is the most powerful for three reasons –

i. It is all consuming in that no area of our lives is immune from its influence or demands.
ii. It affects those of all ages. Both young and old can be ensnared in its beguiling web.
iii. It caters to our need of security. The most demanding need human beings face.

Unfortunately, becoming a member of the Kingdom of God does not immediately release us from its hold. We need to deal ruthlessly with its demands on us, but more on this later.

Verse 15 shows us Jesus' response to the Pharisees, 'You are the ones who justify yourselves.' Money has that power on us. We become uncomfortable whenever we are challenged about our use of it. Such is its hold, that it will often keep us from facing the truth. Rather than doing this we would prefer to justify ourselves. Jesus told this parable in order to illustrate what a powerful resource money is. Such was the deception of the Pharisees that they missed the whole point and attempted instead to soothe their troubled consciences. How often do we respond in similar ways when confronted with this issue?

Jesus goes on to say that what people value highly (ie money), God detests. He then immediately launches into a statement about the Kingdom of God, saying, 'The Law and the prophets were proclaimed until John. Since that time the good news of the Kingdom of God is being preached and people are grabbing the opportunity' (Lk 16:16). We see that the use of money and possessions is intimately linked to the way we live in the Kingdom of God.

What a disturbing illustration Jesus told that day. Money!! It's unrighteous mammon! It can compete directly with God Himself for our allegiance! People can become obsessed with it and justify themselves because of the way that they handle it! God detests the love of it! However, it can be a powerful resource for the Kingdom of God. It can be used shrewdly. We are to effectively utilise it to bring people into God's Kingdom.

The questions is, 'How well is the Christian Church doing in utilising this resource for the Kingdom of God?'

Estimates by David Barrett (International Bulletin 15 of Missionary Research, Vol 12, No 1, January 1988) indicate that the personal income for all Christians around the world during 1988 was 8,201 billion dollars. Total giving to Christian causes that year amounted to 145 billion dollars and of this amount global missions received 8 billion dollars.

Putting it another way – for every $10 that Christians earned 17 cents went to God. Of this 17 cents, 1 cent finished up outside the country of origin – being given to foreign missions. This means that of the 1.7% of our total income given back to God, we spend 17 times more of this on ourselves, in our own countries, than we do meeting the needs overseas. We pour money into our programmes and build impressive church buildings. Despite the millions of dollars we spend in the West, the Church is largely declining or stagnating.

Yet in many non-western countries Christianity is expanding at phenomenal rates. However the shortage of finances in these countries is severely limiting a fuller impact of this expansion.

It is clear that the Christian Church is not being very shrewd!! To be giving only 1.7% of our total earnings to God is miserly to the extreme. To be spending 17 times more on our own spiritual needs than on the enormous needs overseas must be an outright crime. Most of this fault clearly lies with Western-world Christians as they have the greatest earning power. It is obvious that something is very wrong and the work of God languishes because of the selfishness of affluent Christians.

What could be done if we released more money to the Kingdom of God? Could we make a greater impact than at present? There is obviously much room for improvement, the potential is there. The words of Jesus come echoing down through the centuries, 'If you have not been trustworthy in handling worldly wealth, who will trust you with true riches?'

Something is very wrong

* 250,000 people go blind each year for the want of 10 cents worth of vitamin C.
* 40,000 children around the world die each year from the lack of simple needs.
* 100,000,000 children around the world are living on the streets today.
* One billion people around the world are destitute.
* The 37 poorest countries in the world have recently been forced to make a 50% cut in health and a 25% cut in education because of the high interest rates to the West.
* Half the world goes to bed hungry each night.
* By the year 2000, one quarter of the world's population will be living in city slums or squatter settlements.
* North Americans consume 5 times more grain than Asians; use twice as much protein than their bodies need and 80 million of them are overweight!
* One quarter of the world's population controls four fifths of its resources. Putting it the other way, three quarters of the world's population has to get by on one fifth of the world's resources.
* 6% of the world's population consume 40% of its resources and many of these are non-renewable.

Is this what God intended when He put men and women on this planet?

Would we be experiencing such a situation if Christ was ruling this planet now? Will the coming Kingdom of God be like this?

If the answer to these questions is 'No,' then Christians must face up to the shocking injustices staring us in the face from all around this planet. Addressing this topic must come as a direct consequence of our Lord's command to 'Seek first the Kingdom of God.' This very statement of Jesus was framed within the context of a discussion about money and possessions (Matt 6:19-34). If it is God's final intention to right all injustice, then it must be part of our agenda here and now.

God's Perspective on Money and Material Possessions

God has recorded His concern about the use of money and material possessions throughout the whole of Scripture.

1. At Creation

There are four very clear statements made by God to Adam and Eve which are a starting point for our understanding of God's desires regarding this material world.

i. Conservation

God commanded Adam and Eve to 'be fruitful and increase in number to replenish the earth' (Gen 1:28). In this statement we see God's concern regarding future generations. They were to make sure that the human species was conserved and survived. Survival of the race of course depends not only on reproduction but also on the careful use of the environment.

ii. Exploration

Adam and Eve were also to 'subdue' the earth. We have tended to view this command of God in terms of the domination of both animate and inanimate parts of God's creation. There is more to this concept. It is the idea of mastering, understanding and exploring God's creation. This is God's mandate to 'scientists' to seek to discover more about the organisation and functioning of His handiwork. It is God's encouragement to men and women everywhere to investigate and discover for themselves the beauty and order of all He has made.

iii. Administration

Men and women were also to 'rule over' God's creation. They were placed in charge and expected to be faithful managers. Clearly, any exploitation of God's creation was not part of God's intention for this planet.

iv. Co-operation

In Genesis 2:15 God puts Adam in the garden and instructs him to 'dress, and keep it.' God's desire was that men and women should co-operate with Him in the growing of plants and the cultivation of the ground. God would provide the life and growth, people would provide the work.

Work is not a Protestant ethic. It is a mandate of the Kingdom of God. The intention of God was that work should be a creative, fulfilling enterprise. God 'worked' in His creative endeavours (Gen 2:2) and gained great satisfaction in what He did. When He finished His creative activity, 'He saw that it was very good' (Gen 1:31).

The problem with work after the fall is that so much of it has become repetitious and boring. God said to Adam that the ground would be cursed, he would have painful toil and be forced to work by the sweat of his brow (Gen 3:17-19). Unfortunately this is the situation today, thousands of people are locked into drudgery and demeaning labour.

We see that God's intention was that people should conserve the human species, explore His handiwork, administrate the planet and co-operate with Him in the use and handling of the resources of the material world. His desire was that every human being should have equal access to His bountiful provision. There was to be no selfishness, greed, covetousness, laziness, hoarding or exploitation in the Kingdom of God.

God could have made certain that men and women acted responsibly in this regard by controlling them and forcing them to do His bidding, but He gave them the freedom of choice. If a parent brings home some sweets for the children, there are two ways the parent can distribute the sweets to the children. Either the parent personally supervises the handing out of them, ensuring that each child gets a fair share, or the parent can hand all the sweets to the children and tell them to share them out amongst themselves. God chose the latter method when it came to entrusting the material assets of His creation to men and women. However, the advent of sin has meant that people have become self-centred and this has lead to exploitation and greed becoming the trade marks of the management of this planet.

2. In the Nation of Israel

As we have seen earlier, God's desire was for the nation of Israel to model His ways to the surrounding nations.

According to the laws He gave to Israel, every fifty years all land should be returned to the original owners. The land was God's (Lev 25:23) and He gave it to people to meet the needs of the community as a whole, it was not just for personal gain. Every seventh year all slaves were to be set free (Deut 15:12-15). Tithing was required of the Jews. For those who owned lands, the permitting of gleaning in the fields was mandatory. Further, no interest was to be charged on money loaned to fellow Israelites.

Enshrined in these laws given to Israel we see God's intentions. He owned everything. Justice required that everybody had the right to share in God's provision. There was to be no exploitation, no extremes of wealth or poverty and nobody was to be disadvantaged.

Such mechanisms were meant to ensure that the rich didn't simply keep getting richer, and the poor, poorer. It did not mean that God required equality down to the last cent between people. But these laws make it abundantly clear that God never meant gross inequality either.

God promised His ancient people that if they followed His decrees and obeyed His commands they would have rain, crops, harvests, food, peace, protection and His presence (Lev 26:3,13). It is interesting to note that Jesus made a strikingly similar offer to His followers in Matthew 6:19-34. It seems that living by Kingdom principles means that we will know Kingdom provision and Kingdom security.

In Deuteronomy chapter 17 God foreshadows the fact that His people would ask for a king. Clear instructions were given that the king 'must not acquire great numbers of horses for himself . . . He must not take many wives . . . He must not accumulate large amounts of silver and gold' Deut 17:16-17). This was the way that heathen kings lived and again God was looking for a different model. Solomon's heart was led away from God because of his many wives (1 Kings 11:1-4), and his acquiring of material possessions proved to be a futile exercise, as Ecclesiastes 2:1-11 so clearly shows.

The Old Testament record shows that when people became wealthy, they very frequently left God out of their lives, became lazy, corrupt, complacent, unjust and turned to oppression of the poor.

Unfortunately the nation of Israel, and its kings, were no more successful in using God's provision of material resources in a responsible manner than are the majority of Christians today.

3. Through the Old Testament Prophets

Frequently the prophets of the Old Testament warned the people of God, that the way they were handling money and material possessions angered God.

Amos 5:11 'You trample on the poor and force him to give you grain. Therefore, though you have built stone mansions you will not live in them'.

Amos 7:11 'Woe to those who lie upon beds of ivory and stretch themselves upon their couches.'

Is 1:23 'They all love bribes and chase after gifts.'

Jer 5:27 'Like cages full of birds, their houses are full of deceit; they have become rich and powerful and have grown sleek and fat.'

Is 3:18 'In that day the Lord will snatch away their finery: the bangles and the headbands and crescent necklaces, the earrings and bracelets and veils . . . '

Is 5:8 'Woe to those who join house to house, who add field to field, until there is no more room . . . Surely many houses shall be desolate, large and beautiful houses, without inhabitant.'

Hag 1:6 'You have planted much, but have harvested

little. You eat, but never have enough. You drink, but never have your fill. You put on clothes, but are not warm. You earn wages, only to put them in a purse with holes in it.'

Amos 8:5-6 'Skimping the measure, boosting the price and cheating with dishonest scales, buying the poor with silver and the needy for a pair of sandals, selling even the sweepings with the wheat.'

The great cry of the Old Testament prophets about injustice and the way God's people were treating the poor, were very often linked to the use of material possessions and money. After all, the poor are normally poor because they lack essential material requirements and the opportunities to acquire these. Injustice frequently involves the ways in which people gain their wealth.

Not only was God angry about the way many people were becoming rich but He commanded His people to share what they had with others. Isaiah picked this theme up when he said, 'Share your food with the hungry . . . provide the poor wanderer with shelter . . . when you see the naked, clothe him (Is 58:7).

Again we have to conclude that because so much of our life is spent in acquiring, using and looking after material possessions, God spends a great deal of time warning of their dangers and urging that His people use this resource wisely and for others.

4. Through John the Baptist

John the Baptist ushered in the ministry of Jesus with a demand for repentance because the Kingdom of God was at hand. He followed this with a call for the fruit of repentance to be seen in people's lives in economic terms. This fruit was enunciated in terms of money and material possessions. 'The man with two tunics should share . . . the one who has food to do the same . . . don't collect more tax than you should . . . don't extort money . . . be content with your pay' (Lk 3:8-14). True repentance and life in the Kingdom of God demands generosity, justice and contentment. Each of these are expressed in terms of material possessions and money.

5. In the teaching and life of Jesus

Jesus spent a lot of time talking about money and material possessions. Twelve out of 38 parables deal with this topic. One verse in every 10 in Matthew, Mark and Luke deal with it. If we take Luke by itself, then it is one verse in every 7. Jesus spoke much more frequently about this topic than He did about sexual immorality or for that matter any other single issue.

Jesus' views on this subject are very different to those of us brought up with a Western view of money and possessions. His statements are radical and very unsettling to us, living with the lifestyles that we have grown accustomed to. Here are some of them –

Matt 5:40.	If a man sues you and takes your coat, also give him your cloak.
Matt 5:42.	Give to him that asks you.
Matt 6:24.	You can't serve God and Money.
Matt 6:31.	Take no thought for tomorrow . . . for food, drink, clothing.
Matt 10:10.	Disciples were not to provide money, clothes, sandals when they went out with the gospel.
Matt 10:39.	He who loses his life for my sake will find it.
Matt 16:24.	If you want to follow me you must deny yourself and take up your cross.
Matt 16:26.	If you gain the whole world and lose your own soul – that's of no profit.
Matt 19:21.	To the rich young ruler – go and sell your possessions and give to the poor.
Matt 19:23.	Hard for the rich to enter the Kingdom of God.
Lk 6:24-25.	Woe to the rich, woe to the well fed.
Lk 6:30.	Give to those who ask you. If anyone takes what belongs to you, do not demand it back.
Lk 6:34-35.	Lend to those who cannot repay. Love and lend to enemies. There is great reward in this.
Lk 12:15.	Beware of covetousness. A man's life does not consist in the abundance of his possessions.

Lk 12:20.	The man who built bigger barns to store more was called a fool.
Lk 12:33.	To His disciples – sell what you have and give alms.
Lk 14:12.	When giving a dinner, don't invite friends or rich neighbours – they might invite you back. Invite the poor, crippled, lame, blind – you will be blessed, they can't repay.
Lk 14:33.	Whoever does not renounce all he has cannot be my disciple.

Looking at such a list through the eyes of people accustomed to an affluent lifestyle, a consumer-driven economy and an advertising-manipulated society, we are inclined to say, 'Unreasonable. He didn't really mean this. We cannot be expected to live that way today.' We explain these portions away and can very easily find ways to excuse ourselves. But what did Jesus mean? He certainly modelled what He taught. 'Foxes have holes, birds of the air have nests but the Son of Man has nowhere to lay his head,' He said (Lk 9:58). What would He say about our society if He were here today?

We believe in a form of 'passive availability.' We say everything belongs to God. However He would probably have to strike us with lightning to prise us loose from our possessions and money!! Jesus did not teach 'passive availability.' He taught 'active redistribution.' This does not mean that businessmen should necessarily give away business capital. Clearly such finance is necessary for the successful running of a company or business. I believe Jesus was primarily talking about personal finances. He was not suggesting some form of communism, nor was it a political message. It is what the heart of the Father is like and is how His Kingdom functions.

6. In the New Testament Church

The giving of the Holy Spirit at Pentecost, the preaching of the Apostles and the conversion of many into the Christian faith during the early days of the Church sparked an outpouring of generosity among the Christians. We read –

'They shared things in common' (Acts 2:42).
'They had close fellowship, shared belongings and distributed to those in need (Acts 2:44).
'They had meals together' (Acts 2:46).
'They had one mind and heart, no one said their belongings were their own and they shared everything they had' (Acts 4:32).
'No one in the group had need' (Acts 4:34).
'Money was distributed to each according to need' (Acts 4:35).

This was an amazing demonstration of sharing, generosity and contributing to those in need. Surely this was part of the fulfilment of Jesus' message that the gospel would be 'good news to the poor.'

If modern congregations could demonstrate just a little of this type of commitment to each other, what a testimony it would be to those around us. We do these verses, and the early Church, a grave injustice by dismissing this as some sort of wild misguided enthusiasm. Surely this is closer to the heart of God and the ways of His Kingdom than our self-centred, profligate lifestyles.

Warnings about riches and materialism

They prevent entry to the Kingdom of God.
Jesus said it is hard for the rich to enter the Kingdom of God (Lk 18:24-25). Maybe it is also hard for rich Christians to enter more fully into the ways of the Kingdom.

They strangle our growth in the Kingdom of God.
We read in Matthew 13:22 that the seeds (these are the message of the Kingdom, v19) sown in among the thorns were choked. The choking agents are the cares of this world and the deceitfulness of riches. This is a very serious statement. By definition, to be deceived, means we do not know that it is happening to us. I am reminded of a friend who was once talking to third world Christians about the wealth and possessions that Christians in the West had. He told me how appalled they were that Western Christians were able to live

the way they lived in the face of the teaching of the New Testament. How can we do it? Is it that we are deceived?

They blind us to the needs of others.

The rich man passed Lazarus sitting at his gate day after day and apparently did very little to help him. Jesus said Lazarus was covered with sores and longed to eat what fell from the rich man's table. Apparently the rich man was blind to the poor man's needs. (Luke 16-19-31)

They compete directly against God's authority in our lives.

We cannot serve God and Money. Either we will love the one and hate the other or we will be devoted to the one and despise the other. (Lk 16:13).

They enslave our affections.

In Luke 16:14 we read that the Pharisees sneered at Jesus. They loved money, in fact their love had been enslaved by money.

They supplant true values.

Jesus said a person's life does not consist in the abundance of the things he possesses (Lk 12:15). We do not possess life by possessing things, despite what the advertisements tell us and most of us believe.

They create worry and anxiety.

We are told not to worry about what we will eat or drink. That's what the pagan world does (Lk 12:29-34).

They desensitize us towards our own spiritual needs.

The Laodicean church said that they were rich and increased with goods but they didn't know that they were poor, wretched, naked and blind (Rev 3:17).

They are addictive.

Jesus said, 'Watch out, be on your guard against all kinds of greed.' He then went on to tell the story of the man who wasn't content with what he had but planned to pull down his barns to build bigger ones (12:15-21). Money arouses desires that can never be satisfied. Ecclesiastes 5:10 says 'Whoever loves money never has money enough; whoever loves wealth is never satisfied with his income.'

Other New Testament teaching

1. What about tithing?

Tithing is not a New Testament teaching. It is endorsed only once in the New Testament. If it were to be the main expression of giving in New Testament times then Paul would surely have mentioned it in his teaching on giving in 2 Corinthians 8 and 9.

The problem with tithing is that it does not deal with the lust and greed of the human heart. At the best a tithe can only be a good starting point for the Christian.

What is at issue with money and material possessions in the New Testament is not how much I give but how much I keep. Jesus said, 'Don't store up treasure on earth.' Don't keep it! When the widow put in her two mites at the offering in the synagogue, Jesus said she gave all. It was nowhere near as much as the others who had thrown in their money, but she had kept nothing.

The problem in talking this way is that people will inevitably say that others do not know how much they give. This is, of course, true. What we do get an indication of, however, is how much people keep by observing the way they live. This is also what a watching world can see as they observe our lifestyle. By and large our lifestyles are not much different to theirs. How different to the way Jesus and the early Christians lived.

2. The use of the word 'riches'

The Greek word for riches in the New Testament is *ploutos*. This term and its various derivatives are recorded 69 times. Thirty of these references do not refer to material possessions. We read that a person is 'rich in faith' (James 2:5), we should be 'rich to good works' (1 Tim 6:18). In five of these references the word is used in a neutral sense, very often describing a person. We read that Joseph of Arimathea 'was a rich man' (Matt 27:57). In thirty-two of the references the word rich/riches is used in a negative context. We read that 'the rich are sent away empty' (Lk 1:53), 'they that be rich fall into temptation' (1 Tim 6:9), 'the deceitfulness of riches' (Matt 13:22), 'trust not in uncertain riches' (1 Tim 6:17).

This leaves just two references where this word is used in a positive context. We read, 'You will be made rich in every way so that you can be generous on every occasion, and through us your generosity will result in thanksgiving to God' (2 Cor 9:11), 'God richly provides us with everything ... so we can be generous and willing to share' (1 Tim 6:17-18).

Out of 34 references to *ploutos* as in the reference to material possessions, only two are within a positive context and that context is one of giving those riches away!! The only good thing that can be said about riches is that they can be given away!! How can we justify our lifestyles in the light of such verses. I am quite convinced that our affluence makes God vomit!! (Rev 3:16).

3. *The Prostitute of Babylon*

Revelation chapters 17 and 18 describe 'Babylon the Great.' As with other prophetic portions of Scripture it is not wise to be dogmatic about the interpretation. However, interpreting the symbolism of this portion in the light of an end time economic system makes interesting reading and may give us some clues as to economic conditions towards the end of the age.

The system described

17:1   Many waters – convey the concept of a worldwide international system.

17:2   Kings – conveys the added idea of governments and powerful people being involved.

17:2   Inhabitants of the earth – linked with 17:15 clearly indicates masses of people being involved.

17:2   Intoxicated – linked to 18:3 speaks of something out of control. How true today with the massive debts many people and countries are running.

17:2   Wine – something that is addictive.

17:2   Adultery – giving themselves to another. Could be linked with serving God or Mammon.

17:3-5 Well-dressed, ornaments – conveys the idea of

	being very attractive.
17:5	Golden cup full of abominations – full of corruption and injustice.
17:6	Drunk with the blood of saints – such a system destroys the vitality of the people of God.
18:2	Home of demons – demonically controlled.
18:3	Merchants grow rich – source of the world's wealth.
18:3	Excessive luxuries – produces a terrible imbalance.
18:10	City of power – this system is a very powerful one controlling many people.
18:12	Cargoes of gold, precious stones, pearls, fine linen – indicates that such a system contains much wealth and affluence. It also has the control of many commodities.
18:15	Merchants gained their wealth from her – it creates wealthy private individuals.
18:17	Sea captains and sailors – requires the transport of goods internationally.

The system destroyed.

18:8	Plagues will overtake – an imbalance (plague) will destroy this system.
18:8-9	Death, mourning, famine, weeping and terror – this destruction will create great distress.
18:10	In one hour – this destruction will be sudden, surprising and with no warning of a fall (also 18:17,19). With the computer age, stock markets and interdependence of national currencies such a sudden disaster is not beyond our imagination.

It needs to be emphasised again that we cannot categorically state that this prophecy is referring to an economic system but the symbolism is very suggestive. Many of the aspects of the effects of materialism and money discussed earlier in this chapter may be being described in this picture.

What should be our response?

In the light of all we have discussed, what should be the response of those committed to seeking first the Kingdom of God?

A sadly underemphasised aspect of Christian life, particularly in the West, is the whole area of discipleship and its allied topics of commitment and sacrifice.

Many Western Christians live as if we are here to have one long party. Prosperity teaching has not helped. They seek to satiate themselves with all the pleasures, leisure-time activities, modern conveniences, money-making openings, travel opportunities and variety of material possessions that a consumer-driven society parades before them. But we are not here to have a party. At the moment it's war time. The party comes later!!

Many of us have yet to discover the deeper implications of Paul's instructions to Timothy 'Endure hardship with us, like a good soldier of Christ Jesus. No-one serving as a soldier gets involved in civilian affairs – he wants to please his commanding officer' (1 Tim 2:3-4). He goes on to say that the athlete competes according to the rules to receive a crown. The hardworking farmer will receive a share of the crops. He (Paul) endured everything for the sake of the elect that they might obtain salvation . . . with eternal glory. If we die with Him we will live with Him. If we endure with Him we will reign with Him (1 Tim 2:5-12). Work now, rewards later. Endurance now, enjoyment later. Death now, life later. The message is clear, but how often it falls on deaf ears when it is spoken to materialistic, twentieth century Christians.

I do not claim that the answers to this problem are easy, they are not. However we must address them. Here are some simple principles, gleaned from various sources, that some of us have found helpful.

1. *Live more simply*

There are two ways to have enough. One is to acquire more and the other is to live with less. The second is thoroughly Biblical. It was the way Jesus lived and is within the reach of all of us. Living with less is often called living more simply.

If we all decided to live more simply how much finance could we release for the Kingdom of God? What would happen if everyone in our congregations accepted a personal minimum standard of living and poured everything else into the Kingdom of God? The following illustration should demonstrate how unthinkingly we often adopt the ways of this world. What happens to us if we receive an increase in salary of $100 a week? Most of us would have probably adjusted our lifestyle to the previous salary and been seeking to live within it. Now we have an increase, 'Great we can get the extra things we have been wanting.' So after giving 10% to God we enhance our lifestyle to accommodate the extra that we are earning. Is such a response one of discipleship and sacrifice? Is this why God has given us the ability to earn money? Why can't we redirect the whole $100 of extra salary to God?

We are constantly being pressured to 'improve' our standard of living. In fact the economies of the West can only survive if this happens. I believe that we need to commit ourselves to at least holding our personal standard of living in check. Living simply requires discipline, commitment, sacrifice and self-control in the face of a hedonistic, materialistic and self-indulgent society.

We have no doubt often heard sermons on self-control. It is a fruit of the Spirit of God (Gal 5:22). Most of us think of self control in the context of not getting angry. We seldom hear this concept used when it comes to our use of possessions but for many of us it is much more appropriate in this context than in the context of anger.

We need to be able to simplify our lifestyle without getting legalistic about it. Without scoring ourselves against somebody else, getting proud of our achievements and critical of theirs. I must not question somebody else's lifestyle (unless they ask me), I am to question my own lifestyle.

A real problem in seeking to simplify our lifestyles is that today's values will be obsolete tomorrow. What is simple lifestyle today will not be simple lifestyle tomorrow. Luxuries today become necessities tomorrow. However this should not be used as an argument against simplifying our lifestyle any more than society should justify declining moral standards by saying things are different today than they were yesterday. We are called to resist the process of decay which is occurring within our society.

Nor does living simply mean we should be miserable by being frugal. Frugality without liberality achieves nothing.

Being miserly towards ourselves without being generous towards others is not what God wants. Living simply should not so much be an emphasis on what I don't do, but what I do do.

Jesus lived simply when He came to earth. He stepped down from the splendour of heaven to the sinfulness of earth. He owned very little. If He earned anything as a carpenter, He certainly had not saved any for His ministry. I am not suggesting that we should live exactly like Him. He was not a family man and His ministry only spanned three years. What I am suggesting is that His example should be the one we consider, rather than the ones we see around us or those that are presented to us on television.

John Wesley as a young man, calculated that he only needed £28 a year to take care of his needs. At the time he made that decision he was earning £30 a year. He lived on £28 a year for the rest of his life even though some years he was earning round about fourteen hundred pounds a year. In other words, he was living on 50 times less than what he was earning. He used to say to his followers, 'Gain all you can, save all you can, give all you can.'

It is very difficult to seek to establish a simpler lifestyle once a more lavish one has been established and particularly so if one has teenage children!! Every young couple embarking on marriage should discuss this matter before they marry and have children. They should decide before God that they will not be seduced by the society around them. That they will live within their means and seek to pour as much finance back into God's Kingdom as possible.

2. *Resist advertising and develop sales resistance*

The modern retail industry is geared first to getting us into situations (mainly shops) where we can see, smell, taste and otherwise experience its merchandise. After that the aim is to separate us from as much of our money as possible before we leave the premises. The choice of colour for packaging is a scientific exercise. Certain colours enhance the possibility of sales of various items. Stores are laid out in strategic ways to help us spend our money. Soft music plays to soothe the senses. Billions of dollars are spent each year on advertising, trying to con us that Jesus was wrong when He said, 'Watch out! Be on your guard against all kinds of greed; a man's life does not consist in the abundance of his possessions.' Most of the time, advertising is not in our best interests but in the interests of the seller. It is designed to create desire and greed. Greed always exceeds need. Not only does advertising delude us, but if we fall for it we also finish up paying for it with the product we are purchasing. The 'lust of the eyes' is not just to do with adultery. Satan was the first advertising man. At the fall he geared his attack towards Eve by appealing to pride, 'You will be like God' (Gen 3:4). The fruit appealed to Eve's senses, 'It was good for food and pleasing to the eye' and also towards her desire for status, it was 'desirable for gaining knowledge' (Gen 3:6). Appealing to pride, senses and status is at the heart of the advertising industry today.

How can a person be paid $1,000,000 for winning a tennis tournament or $10,000,000 for winning the heavy weight boxing title of the world? It's immoral! To argue that this is value for money and it's just using market forces doesn't make it right. The only way these amounts can be earned for such activities is by utilising advertising. It is absolutely essential that we develop sales resistance, model it to our families, encourage each other to maintain vigilance and warn people against it from our pulpits.

3. Reject credit

Not only does advertising seek to separate us from our money and incessantly stimulate us to spend more and more on non essential items, but it demands that we must have that item now.

'If you can't afford it that doesn't matter. We will finance it for you,' and so we finish paying up to 30% more for instant gratification. There used to be a day when if you couldn't afford something you didn't get it. That day seems to be long gone. Christians are only too happy to borrow into financial bondage, becoming just as much slaves to the financial moguls as the negroes were to the cotton plantation owners of the Southern States.

Oh for a generation of Christian young people who rise up and say 'Enough of this frenzy.' Could this happen? Don't hold your breath. Young people do not have many adult models to follow in this regard.

4. Budget carefully

Budgeting is nothing more than planning for the future. Jesus told a parable about this when He spoke of the person who was going to build a tower first sitting down to count the cost (Luke 14:28-32). There is a common misconception about budgeting, that it is only needed for those who are struggling to make ends meet. Obviously budgeting helps such people. However, it seems that budgeting is just as important for those who have more money than they need. In this situation it is easy to fritter away valuable resources and not be disciplined in our approach to handling finance. We need to work within a framework which says, 'Lord, after covering our basic needs, whatever is left over we are going to either give to You or utilise for You.'

5. Give regularly, joyfully and generously to God and others

The New Testament is quite clear about this. The Corinthian church was encouraged to give regularly, 'On the first day of each week, each one of you should set aside a sum of money in keeping with his income' (1 Cor 16:2). We know that 'God loves a cheerful giver' (2 Cor 9:7). Paul says the Macedonian churches gave joyfully and generously 'out of the most severe trial, their overwhelming joy and their extreme poverty welled up in rich generosity' (2 Cor 8:2). We read that if we 'sow generously we will reap generously' (2 Cor 9:6); we will 'be made rich so as you can be generous . . . your generosity will result in thanksgiving to God' (2 Cor 9:11); we are to be generous and willing to share' (1 Tim 6:18).

Tony Campolo has reminded us that the most profane thing we can do with money is to give it away. It's against its laws, it destroys its value to us, causes grace to penetrate its system and undermines its competitive nature. As mammon competes directly with God for the attention of the human heart, to give money to God is profanity par excellence.

6. Abandon the wrong use of possessions

Don't buy things for status.

Many of the things our society offers us are simply to enable us to project a certain image and this caters to snobbery. Certain brands of cars, houses in desirable locations and clothing are the most obvious in this area. Paul told Timothy to 'command those who are rich in this world not to be arrogant about their wealth' (1 Tim 6:17). Someone has said that snobbery is spending money you don't have, to buy things you don't need, to impress people you don't like! I am not suggesting that Christians should be frumpy and dowdy. But we do not have to follow in lemming-like manner the dictates of the fashion world and its incestuous partner, the media, which are geared to the stimulation of covetousness and greed. In general it's a good rule to buy things for their practicality rather than their looks. Remember – a car is just a four-wheeled, labour-saving and time-saving device. For a Christian, it should not be purchased as some sort of a status symbol.

Don't buy things for security.

Jesus said, 'Don't store up for yourself treasure on earth' (Matt 6:19). Earthquakes, fire, inflation, stock crashes, governmental economic decisions, and the collapse of financial institutions are the modern moths and rust. Biblical faith does not seek its security in possessions or money but in God. Jesus said it's the pagans who run after these things (Matt 6:32) not the children of His Kingdom. Christians should have a carefree (not careless) attitude when it comes to material possessions and money. Three times in the latter verses of Matthew 6 Jesus says 'Don't worry' (Matt 6:25,27,28). God's desire is that His people have freedom from anxiety.

Don't buy things for selfish ambition.

Jesus said, 'Watch out, be on your guard against all kinds of greed, a person's life does not consist in the abundance of their possessions' (Lk 12:15).

There are several warnings about covetousness in the New Testament. It is equated with idolatry (Col 3:5). It is listed among the sins of those whom God has given over to sexual impurity (Rom 1:24-32). It was the basic motive that caused the fall. All of us in one way or another are affected by covetousness.

Covetousness is a desire to have more than we need, while greed is keeping more than I need. A person who is hungry does not covet food. It would be a wrong use of the word in such a context. It is not wrong to desire a basic need but it is wrong to desire more than we require. The problem facing us in the West is that we are constantly demanding higher standards of living while one billion people go to bed hungry each night. For us, the main issue is not making a living but maintaining a lifestyle!

The opposite of the concept of covetousness is the concept of being content (contentment) and this also occurs several times in the New Testament and simply means to be satisfied or have sufficient. If we have food and clothing we are to be content (1 Tim 6:6-10). We are to keep our lives free from the love of money and be content with what we have (Heb 12:5). Paul said he knew what it was to have need and plenty. But he had learned the secret of being content in any and every situation, whether fed or hungry, living in plenty or want (Phil 4:11-13). We must learn to identify what are our needs and what are our greeds. Contentment is worth achieving. It is God's desire for us and should be a feature of the lifestyle of those in the Kingdom of God.

If we are going to deal with matters involving status, security and selfish ambition in our Western societies, we are going to need to know the ministry of the Holy Spirit and the accountability and support of fellow Christians.

7. Break the cycle

Do we really need all we possess? Probably not. Then why not give something of value away or sell it and give the money away. Jesus suggested to the rich young ruler that he go and sell all he had and give to the poor (Matt 19:21).

For us the call may not be 'sell all' but to at least 'sell some.' In another place Jesus said to His disciples that they should 'sell their possessions and give to the poor' (Lk 12:33). The emphasis of our modern society is 'buy and get.' We need groups of Christians who will reverse this and 'sell and give.'

As a young man at University I can well remember a growing conviction that God wanted me to give my camera, a gift from my parents, to a missionary friend. Over a number of weeks I struggled with this. Photography was something I really enjoyed, but God confirmed this conviction in a number of ways. Finally I said to the Lord that I would give it away provided it was obvious that my missionary friend needed it and I had an opportunity to raise the topic with him. That evening I visited my friend to find him sorting his missionary slides, I had an opportunity to talk about cameras! He told me he had had to sell his camera in India to help pay for his fare home! He needed another camera! He got mine!

This action broke something in me. It broke the longing for material possessions. Such radical action is sometimes needed and for many of us it may well be the fruit of repentance (Lk 3:8-11).

The rich young ruler wasn't prepared to break the cycle and he went away sad. When Jesus saw his response He said, 'It is hard for a rich man to enter the Kingdom of heaven' (Matt 19:23). How many of us as Christians are prevented from fully entering the Kingdom of God because of the material things of life that fill our horizons?

8. *Buy second hand*

A friend of mine once gave me some very sound advice prior to marriage. He said, 'We bought all the furniture for our home second hand and saved ourselves thousands of dollars.' It has proved to be sound advice and I have passed it on to many young couples during pre-marriage counselling. Just taking things off the shop floor and out the door probably depreciates them by 20-30% before they are even used. What a waste of money!

Obviously some items need to be bought new. A second-hand toothbrush is probably pushing this principle too far!!

9. *Remember we are stewards not owners*

Transfer the ownership of all you have to God. It's actually His anyway. After all who gave us the ability to work? Was it our decision that we were born into a country where we were able to earn enough money? Did we choose the natural abilities we possess? Are we totally in control of our health and safety? For a Christian everything they have belongs to

God and they are therefore stewards of all they have.

Two important factors follow from this principle. Firstly, we are responsible to look after the things we have been given. Carelessness with our possessions for a Christian is an affront to our Maker. Secondly, as it belongs to God we can release our material possessions to others for their use. Such action may entail some risk of damage. Having ensured as best we can that the user will be careful with the goods, we then have to trust God that He can look after His stuff.

Someone has said, 'We need to earn much, consume little, give generously, celebrate life.' The world says we celebrate life by earning much, consuming everything (preferably on ourselves), and giving nothing.

Proverbs 30:8-9 is a prayer for every Christian who wants to live faithfully by the principles of the Kingdom of God –

> 'Give me neither poverty nor riches, feed me with food that is convenient for me, lest I be full and deny you and say "who is the Lord?" Or lest I be poor and steal and take the Name of the Lord my God in vain.'

This has got to be both the greatest challenge facing Western Christians, and at the same time, their greatest opportunity.

May God give us all fresh insights into the potential and the pitfalls as we seek to grapple with this topic.

We will finish this chapter with the same quote with which we commenced it .

> *'"Good news to the poor," means that every person has a right to as much of the material things as will make them mentally, spiritually and physically fit for the purposes of the Kingdom of God, the rest belongs to the needs of others.'*
> E Stanley Jones.

CHAPTER TWELVE

THE CHURCH AND THE KINGDOM OF GOD

I had just finished teaching about the Church and the Kingdom of God when a woman came up to talk to me. I could tell by the look on her face that what I had been saying had encouraged her. Breathlessly she thrust out her hand to shake mine and expressed her gratitude. The conversation went something like this –

'You've no idea how much that helped me,' she said. 'I have been working for some time in a Citizens Advice Bureau. I know God has called me to do this work, I prayed about it a lot before I accepted the position. I've been able to direct people coming to the Bureau to Christian people for help, prayed with some people and recently I led someone to the Lord. A week or two ago I felt I should talk to my Pastor, tell him what I was doing and get his "covering".'

Her pastor's response – 'What are you doing that for? That's not helping our church!!'

'After hearing you I know that what I felt the Lord has been saying to me was correct, I'm so happy' and with that she turned and walked away.

I was left standing at the front of the auditorium in amazement. To think that a pastor was not happy with this woman for wanting to get involved in the community, and in a front line ministry at that. How sad, but this is unfortunately not the first time that I have encountered such a situation. There are probably hundreds of people in congregations around the world who have experienced a similar rebuff. We pastors can become very possessive when it comes to 'our' church and the participation of people in its activities.

The Church

If it is to the Gospels that we turn to discover something of the teaching of Jesus about the Kingdom of God, then it is to the Epistles and especially the teachings of Paul that we must look for an understanding of the Church. Rather than playing the Gospels off against the Epistles, as some have done, it is important that we understand the relationship one to the other.

The Greek word most often used to describe the Church in the New Testament is *ekklesia*. Unfortunately in translating this as 'church' we have lost something of the real meaning behind the word. Literally the Greek word means 'the called out ones' and was commonly used in the first century to describe a group of people who had come into a public place for a particular purpose. The Greek version of the Old Testament also sometimes uses the word *ekklesia* to describe the people of Israel. The early Christians used a word indicating a public meeting of some sort, which sharply contrasts with its use today. Now most Church activities are conducted behind closed doors and are not very accessible to the public.

To replace the word 'Church' in the New Testament with the phrase 'the called out ones' is a very constructive exercise. Why did the writers of the New Testament use this word? No doubt the foremost reason was because it identified a group of people (Christians) called out of their homes to a local meeting place. Is it not also possible that it indicated a group of people who had been called out of the kingdom of darkness and called into the Kingdom of God (Col 1:12-13)?

The New Testament recognises three dimensions of the Church. There is the universal Church, the Body of Christ, composed of all believers since Pentecost. We read in Ephesians 5 :23-32, 'Christ is the head of the Church, his body . . . Christ loved the Church and gave himself up for her.' Then there is the local Church. A group of people living in a discreet geographical area at a particular time, for example the church at Corinth (1 Cor 1:2), the churches of Galatia (Gal 1:2). Finally there is an even smaller group of people, those that meet in a house (1 Cor 16:19).

Those of us brought up in evangelical circles have no difficulty in recognising that the Church is primarily people. It is not a denomination, a building or an organisation. It is people who have been born into the Kingdom of God by the redeeming work of Christ on the cross, and the ministry of the Holy Spirit. It has been variously described as the 'new community,' a 'pilgrim people,' the 'Body of Christ,' the 'Messianic community,' or 'God's family and household.'

Thus we can say that the Church is the people of the Kingdom, the community of the King. It is also the servant or agent of the Kingdom. Yeast is an agent in bread making; it's the active ingredient that causes the dough to rise. It is in this sense that the Church (the people of the Kingdom) is an ingredient – one of God's ingredients to achieve His Kingdom purposes today.

The Church is an essential part of God's programme at this time on this planet. Ephesians 3:10 gives us an incredible picture of the part it plays in God's current purposes – 'His intent was that now, through the Church, the manifold wisdom of God should be made known to the rulers and authorities in the heavenly realms.' That God's multi-faceted wisdom should be demonstrated here and now to angelic and demonic hosts through such a group of imperfect people, is an almost unbelievable thing.

Is the Church the Kingdom?

From the above discussion it should be clear that this is not so. Although we enter both the Church and the Kingdom of God at conversion this does not mean that they are identical. A pupil entering a High School in this country as a student for the first time, normally commences in the third form, but the third form is not the High School neither is the High School the third form, they are distinct identities. So it is for the Church and the Kingdom.

The Kingdom of God is a much larger identity than the Church but it embraces the Church (Figure 4). In trying to illustrate this point further, the Kingdom of Tonga (probably the closest kingdom to our country) comes to mind. The Kingdom of Tonga is more than just the people of Tonga. It includes their politics, their economics, their relationships, their land and their possessions. So it is with the Kingdom of God. It is obviously more than just the people. In fact the Kingdom of God has identity and existence quite apart from the presence or absence of human beings. We can say that the Kingdom of God is at work in the Church but it is also above and beyond it.

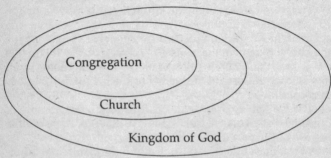

Figure 4. Relationship of Kingdom of God to Church & congregation

Neither can we substitute the word Kingdom in many passages of Scripture for the word Church, or vice versa, and still make sense of that passage. Christ died to redeem the Church, He didn't die to redeem the Kingdom. God's Kingdom doesn't need redeeming, the Kingdom of God is itself redemption.

We could describe churches (ie congregations = 'church' with a little 'c') as colonies of the Kingdom of God here and now. They are supposed to be credible witnesses to the love, justice and mercy of God to the surrounding communities. God has chosen the Church to model something of His Kingdom purposes to a watching world. It is rather salutary to describe our congregations as colonies and my fear is that we fall a long way short of God's expectations. However it is certainly a goal that we should be setting ourselves.

In response to Peter's affirmation that Jesus was the Christ, the Son of the Living God, Jesus says, 'On this rock I will build my church . . . I will give you the keys of the

Kingdom' (Matt 16:13-19). Jesus would build the Church and He gave to His followers the keys of the Kingdom. By our actions, we have tended to reverse these two statements. We have often over-emphasised the church and under-emphasised the Kingdom. We have in effect said, 'Lord we will build the Church and you look after the Kingdom.' Keys are often seen as a mark of authority. To have the keys to a building gives that person authority over the building, to let people in and decide how it should be used. So Christ has given His followers authority within His Kingdom.

Congregations

One of the problems with our Western Christianity is that we have given an enormous amount of time, thought, effort and money to the church – to the neglect of the Kingdom of God. The truth is that the Kingdom of God is a much larger canvas for us to paint on.

Peter Wagner speaking about the Kingdom of God makes the following point.

> *'I cannot help wondering out aloud why I have not heard more about it in the thirty years that I have been a Christian? I certainly have read about it enough in the Bible . . . But honestly I cannot remember any pastor whose ministry I have been under actually preaching a sermon on the Kingdom of God. As I rummage through my own sermon barrel, I now realise that I myself have never preached a sermon on it. Where has the Kingdom been?'*

(From – 'Church Growth & the Whole Gospel', page 2, – published by Marc, Europe, 1981.)

We have tended to make the church (congregation) an end in itself, when God meant it to be a means to an end. Part of the mission of the Church is to seek to bring people, structures and things under the rule of Christ. God's final goal is to unite all things in Christ (Eph 1:10) and to reconcile all things to Himself through Christ (Col 1:20). Until God ushers in the time when this will be complete and final, the Church is to engage in the task of an agent of reconciliation (2 Cor 5:17-21). The Church is to be both evangelistic and prophetic in its witness to the Kingdom of God, to proclaim and demonstrate the rule of God. Proclamation without demonstration may just be empty words. In fact demonstration often leads to proclamation and it has been said that one in the eye is better than two in the ear!

So often the local congregation has been the total focus and goal of most Christians' activities. We have concerned ourselves with congregational structures, organisation, finances, our gifts in the church. All these are right and proper in their place, but they have filled our horizons and we have lost the bigger picture – the Kingdom of God. For many people full-time work in the church is often placed on a pedestal and seen as the most important work that a person can be involved in for God. Too great a preoccupation with the congregation has caused people, pastors and ministers in particular, to be very possessive and protective of their people. As we have done this, churches have become inward-looking, isolated and irrelevant to much of society. Many of our congregations have just become 'clubs,' simply catering for the needs of their members.

How careful we have to be during combined church crusades that the converts go to the 'right churches' and that a single congregation or denomination doesn't get all the fish! 'After all, we have put time and money into this effort. We want to make sure that we get something out of it'. Against this a Kingdom of God world view says – 'Wasn't it great that people came to Christ during the crusade. It doesn't matter to us which congregation they attend so long as they are going to be nurtured in Christ.'

Churches and growth

It is unfortunate that Church growth teaching has tended to cause this focus on the congregation to be increased and has further made the church the centre of attention. There are many helpful principles in Church growth teaching but it is possible for congregations and church leaders to fall into worldly ways and become competitive. Such attitudes are counterproductive to the Kingdom of God and make co-operation between congregations very difficult.

I have often wondered why it is that some congregations

regularly advertise in the church notice section of the local newspapers. Is it because the unsaved are anxiously awaiting their newspaper so they can pore over the church notices to see what exciting event is occurring in the local churches this weekend with the intention of rushing off to attend? I think not! It is more likely so that other local Christians can know what exciting events are occurring in our congregation and possibly be attracted to our church – with the view to joining of course! The percentage of non-church people who attend a congregation's service because they have read the church notices must be minuscule. Unfortunately churches spend thousands of dollars of God's money each year trying to attract adherents from other congregations to their own, and then chalk it up as 'Church growth!'

Frequently the goal of congregations is to see how many people they can get! This is not the stated goal; we would not be so blatant as to say that! The question as to how many people attend a certain congregation is a high priority on many people's list of questions about a particular church. Ask any minister or pastor who goes to a church leaders conference! Denominations have their yearly 'stud books' where facts and figures are all recorded. Large and growing numbers in a congregation are often taken as an indication of success. A cursory look at most advertising material for seminars where ministers or pastors are key speakers, will prove this!! I confess that when our congregation was growing rapidly it was nice to count the numbers and draw the graphs. I know that fishermen and shepherds both count, but most of the fishermen that I know, count to boast! For many a young pastor starting out in the ministry a growing congregation is a satisfying goal and they tend to put all their energies to this end.

It needs to be said that a large congregation may have little or no effect within the community and therefore may not be amounting to much in terms of the Kingdom of God in that area. To grow a large congregation is not a Biblical goal; to seek first the Kingdom of God is.

If all Christians associated with a local congregation, committed themselves to 'seeking first the Kingdom of God' and witnessed to the rule and reign of God by demonstration and proclamation in all areas of their lives, then people in local communities would have to consider what it was that made their lives so different. Some may then decide to become part of that Kingdom for themselves. Thus if we seek first the Kingdom of God and our congregation grows, this is a bonus, but it should not be the main goal of a congregation. That goal should be the extension of the rule of God in their local community. We need to set and evaluate all our congregational goals in terms of the Kingdom of God. Our loyalty to a local congregation should only be to the degree that congregation is loyal to the Kingdom of God. Loyalty to church structure, denomination or hierarchy is not the same as commitment to the Kingdom of God.

This is not to down-grade evangelism or the importance of seeing people come to faith in Jesus Christ. Evangelism must have a high priority but the best evangelism comes out of lifestyle – the lifestyle of the Kingdom of God. It is God's intention that we model this to those around us. The Kingdom of God is radically different from, and challenges the fallenness of, the status quo in our society.

Neither am I advocating a dismantling of the congregations. The New Testament shows us that it is God's intention for Christians to gather in groups. The need of the moment is to establish the right balance between an emphasis on the congregation and an emphasis on the Kingdom of God.

Limited congregational time and activities

There are only a limited array of activities that can be undertaken in most local congregations. Mention preaching, youth work, music, deacons and pastoral work and you about cover the extent of most congregations' activities. Where do professions such as medicine, architecture and law, or trades such as building, motor mechanic and plumber, fit in the congregation? Are these just occupations for people to make money? Or is there a possibility that such areas could be used by Christians to minister to a needy community and demonstrate something of the Kingdom of God?

Take for example architects. As professionals, how can their expertise be utilised within a local congregation? Well, no doubt an architect would design that new church building, or the modifications to the old one. But beyond this there is a very limited role for such expertise within the Church. But not so within the Kingdom, as the following illustration will show.

During the mid 1980's, the advent of high interest rates in our country and the flow of people into the cities caused housing prices in the cities to escalate. Young families seeking their first home were particularly hard hit. Several people within the congregation were concerned about this and had been prayerfully considering this housing crisis.

As a result, an architect in the congregation designed an attractive low-cost home. He believes that after more than thirty years in architecture, the Holy Spirit gave him this plan. A Christian builder within the congregation established a trust and a block of land was purchased which was cross-leased. Seventeen families applied to become part of this venture. The first ten to arrange their finance were accepted and the building of ten homes commenced.

Although every home had the same basic design, each family was able to negotiate with the architect the individual features and internal design to suit their needs. In conjunction with the developer, applicants were also able to do as much of their own work on their home as they were able. Costs were kept to a minimum by bulk buying, tendering for sub-contractors and no built-in profit margins for the trust were made.

As a result of this co-operative venture these families were able to obtain their first home with land for around $63,000 each. The average cost for a commercially built home, with land, in our city at this time was $100,000. Such a venture created a great deal of interest in the local community, the local press and the Government. The Housing Minister of the time wrote to the trust asking how the savings had been made and what was the motivation for doing this!!

Such ventures should not be entered into lightly, there are many problems and difficulties. However this illustrates the potential that the Body of Christ has to creatively serve the needs within a local community.

Far too many people sit in church pews dissatisfied with

their Christian experience. They are often unextended in their congregational activities and absorbed in the materialistic culture which surrounds them. To release their talents and creative God-given abilities they often throw themselves into their work, hobbies and sport but with very little purpose other than for their own personal satisfaction and enjoyment. To be sure, in such situations they expect to find opportunities to witness for Christ but there must be more relevance to these areas of life than just evangelism and our own fulfilment.

What does it mean to seek first the Kingdom of God in professional life, in a trade or in any other area of life? There are huge areas of untapped potential, finance, abilities and skills lying underutilized in the people of the Kingdom of God. We must redress this situation by recapturing a vision of the Kingdom of God which embraces all of living.

Not only do we have limited activities in congregational life but we spend a limited amount of time in congregational activities. Out of the 168 hours in a week, most people would be pushed to spend 10 hours a week in congregational activities. What happens to the other 158 hours a week? For too long we have seen the other 158 hours as our 'own time' and with dichotomy between the sacred and the secular have tended to limit our Christian activity to the 'church bit.' A vision of the Kingdom of God, requires that we observe His kingly rule in all things, at all times, in all places and as our highest priority, changes all of this.

What role for the congregation?

We must not separate Church and Kingdom, neither must they be confused as one and the same thing. The work of the Kingdom must be grounded in the community of the King. To disband the congregation is to go against all the teaching of the Epistles.

Why then has God ordained that we come together in groups? There seem to be three main reasons; for **worship**, for **fellowship** and for **equipping**. We see this in the early Church where we read, 'They devoted themselves to the apostles teaching **(equipping)**, to fellowship **(fellowship)** and to praising God' **(worship)**, Acts 2:42-47. We worship the King, we fellowship with other members of the Kingdom and we are equipped to better seek the Kingdom of God in the society in which we live. We need to trim our congregational activities to a bare minimum. Far too much time and money is spent in maintenance activities. We must put a high priority on worship, fellowship and equipping, release our best people to facilitate them and not feel that everybody needs to have a go at something in the congregation in order to achieve spiritual fulfilment.

As we have wrestled with these issues we have come up with a series of propositions upon which we are seeking to build.

In our congregational life we are seeking to –

a. recognise the priority of the Kingdom without losing the significance of the Church

b. reduce congregational activities to the essential minimum and do these well

c. free from congregational activities those who have the call of God on their lives to demonstrate the Kingdom of God in strategic areas in their local communities or nation

d. encourage people to recognise that there are no such categories as 'sacred' (often congregation related) and 'secular' (often non-church related) within the Kingdom of God

e. catch a vision to utilise for the Kingdom of God the huge untapped resources of finance, possessions, abilities and skills of the people of God

f. help God's people find significant and rewarding roles within the congregation and community.

Why renewal?

Over the past 25 years many congregations have seen a genuine work of renewal by the Holy Spirit. Many have come to faith in Christ. People have been filled with the Spirit. Congregations have grown. Spiritual gifts have operated and new expressions of worship have invigorated once lifeless services. The power of God has been seen among His people, and for many there has been a return to prayer and a love for the study of the Word of God. For all this, we must be grateful to God but one is forced to ask the question – 'To what ultimate end has all this occurred?' 'Is it just to bring new life to the local congregation?' 'Was this renewal meant to be encapsulated within the four walls of the local church or did God have a Kingdom purpose in mind?'

Surely God's purpose was to turn Christians out into their communities with the power and love of His Spirit. In doing so to seek to bring His authority and rule to all areas of society and local communities, thereby alerting men and women to the presence of God among His people.

Howard Snyder has this to say:

'The Church gets into trouble whenever it thinks that it is in the church business rather than in the Kingdom business. In the church business, people are concerned with church activities, religious behaviour and spiritual things. In the Kingdom business, people are concerned with Kingdom activities, all human behaviour and everything God has made, visible and invisible. Kingdom people see human affairs saturated with spiritual meaning and Kingdom significance. Kingdom people seek first the Kingdom of God and its justice; church people often put church work above concerns of justice, mercy and truth. Church people think about how to get people into the church; Kingdom people think about how to get the church into the world. Church people worry that the world might change the church; Kingdom people work to see the church change the world. When Christians put the church ahead of the Kingdom, they settle for the status quo and their own kind of people. When they catch a vision of the Kingdom of God, their sight shifts to the poor, the orphan, the widow the refugee, "the wretched of the earth" and to God's future. They see the life and work of the church from the perspective of the Kingdom. If the church has one great need, it is this: To be set free for the Kingdom of God, to be liberated from itself as it has become, in order to be itself as God intends.'

(From – 'Liberating the Church', page 25 – published by IVP, 1983.)

What is needed is a new model of congregational life. A

model that embraces the Kingdom of God yet retains the role of the church. This will be the topic of our next chapter.

CHAPTER THIRTEEN

PUTTING IT ALL TOGETHER

NEEDED – A NEW CONGREGATIONAL MODEL

I was sitting in the lounge of a young couple who were heading up a vital and growing work ministering to surfies. They had been instrumental in establishing Christian surfer's clubs around our country to work among the surfing establishment. People had been converted and young Christians were being encouraged to witness and share with those on the surf beaches around this country. Each year this organisation ran one of the best surfing competitions in the country and used it as an opportunity to share the gospel with hundreds of heathen young people on our beaches.

As I spoke to this young man and his wife I sensed their frustration with the church. They had attended two congregations during the previous five years and in each congregation they felt that the leadership wasn't really interested in what they were doing. In fact in one case they had been told that what they were doing was clearly not of God. The Pastor had asked, 'How could God be interested in Christian young people being involved in such a godless sport as surfing?' They felt unwanted, very lonely and almost a bit dirty. The pressure of the work was great and there seemed to be few in the established church with whom they could share it. Yet this young couple was involved in a vital ministry, seeking to extend the Kingdom of God in a creative and effective way.

Unfortunately many people feel that church leaders are only interested in their own agendas. To a certain degree this is right and proper. God gives leadership the responsibility of leading and setting the direction for a local congregation. Clearly the leadership must seek to ensure that this direction is maintained, thus leaders are keen to encourage people into areas of activity which enhance the work of the congregation. Those in full-time leadership roles in congregations spend a great deal of time thinking, planning and praying about congregational activities. Inevitably they expect others to exhibit the same degree of interest and commitment to these activities. However the rest of the congregation will have very different centres of interest to that of the full-time minister or pastor. Because the centre of the pastor or minister's attention is the church, this will often bring them into tension with people in the congregation who seem to be carrying out activities which will not directly enhance the congregation's life and growth. Such was the case for this young couple involved in evangelising surfies.

A radical change of view is required for many church leaders. We must see the Kingdom of God as our priority and seek to define our goals for the congregation in terms of God's Kingdom, not just the congregation.

Is it possible for the twin concepts of the church and the Kingdom to be held together within a workable framework? Will encouraging people to seek first the Kingdom of God in their local communities leave the congregational activities bereft of support? If we emphasise the congregation, will we lose sight of the Kingdom of God, or if we major on the Kingdom of God, will we destroy the congregation? There is definitely a tension here, it must be recognised and addressed.

I believe that a modified model of the church is urgently needed. Many Christians are becoming increasingly disillusioned with modern church life; its lack of credibility with the community at large; its small-mindedness and lack of vision; its tendency towards navel gazing and its restrictive structures. Many pastors and ministers find themselves carrying loads which are too great for them, pressures are mounting and many are leaving the ministry.

In the past, visionaries have often been forced to go outside the local congregation in order to create effective ministries and some of these have led to the launching of para-church organisations. Such leaders have often seen a need within society, sensed God's call to meet that need, and sought to establish a work to minister to that need. How many such ministries were birthed in a local congregation, shared with the leadership and then dismissed by that leadership because the proposed ministry did not coincide with the leaders' vision or goals?

Since World War II it is estimated that about 6,000 parachurch agencies have been formed in the USA alone. Why could congregations not contain these? Some para-church ministries have become trans-global and of necessity could not be contained within the framework of one local congregation. However, in many cases there has been an unhealthy competition and a considerable amount of suspicion between the local church and para-church ministries.

One could say that the para-church ministries have often had the vision and the local churches have had the people and the resources. All too often churches have lacked vision and para-church ministries have lacked people and resources. Maybe what is needed within local congregations, is the bringing together of the best of the para-church emphasis, of ministering to specific groups, with the strengths of the church's support networks and resources. We need to release people into creative, Holy Spirit inspired ministries, which impact local communities for the Kingdom of God but are based within the support and nurture of active local congregations.

This modified model of the church doesn't draw people out of society into some sort of private club, nor does it seek to dominate society by aiming at positions of power. Rather it equips people to function effectively as servants within the society, reflecting the values of the Kingdom of God to all they come in contact with.

Towards a new congregational model

In seeking to draw together the several threads that we have been exploring in this book I want to suggest that the following features should be part of a new (modified?) congregational model.

i. Embraces a theology of the Kingdom of God

Such a theology will give the congregation a very wide base for activity. It will encourage those in the congregation to seek many opportunities for effective ministry within the local community and overseas. It will integrate the many activities that a congregation is capable of running as well as the various theological emphases that its members hold. By accommodating the tension between the 'already but not yet' aspects of the Kingdom of God, it should shield the congregation from the extremes of pessimism and triumphalism.

ii. Open to the continual renewing work of the Holy Spirit

Such congregations will enthusiastically embrace and seek a deeper and continued renewing ministry of the Holy Spirit. They will be open to receive all the gifts of the Spirit and will recognise that gifts of the Spirit are given not solely to produce a healthy congregation but so as a healthy congregation might seek to bring God's restoring activity to the surrounding society. To be involved in an active role within the Kingdom of God demands submission to and co-operation with, the ministry of the Holy Spirit.

iii. Involved in social concern

All human need offers an opportunity for the manifestation of the power, grace and love of the King, through the compassionate serving of His subjects. Serving is at the heart of the Kingdom message. Jesus made it quite clear that He came not to be served but to serve (Matt 20:28). After talking about serving (Lk 22:25-30) He goes on to say that just as His Father has conferred a Kingdom on Him, so He is conferring one on them. Later they will sit on thrones.

Serving now – ruling later. So it was then for Jesus, thus it is now for His followers.

iv. Committed to evangelism

We unashamedly believe that evangelism means bringing people to that position of loving the Lord their God with all their heart, soul, strength and mind. This is the first and highest commandment. A radical change within the life of each individual is the starting point for permanent change in people and society. The Kingdom rule of God must commence in the lives of individuals if it is to effectively extend into and impact all areas of society.

v. Co-operates with para-church ministries and other local churches

Viewing things from the perspective of the Kingdom of God, should help us to see that our congregations are not the centre of either our goals, or God's goals. To achieve the maximum impact for the Kingdom of God in local communities, it will be absolutely essential for local congregations to co-operate in as many areas as possible. Such co-operation will be the fulfilling of our Lord's prayer in John 17, 'May they also be one so that the world might believe that you have sent me.'

vi. Reduces congregational activities to an essential minimum.

Such a model will see the role of the local congregation from the framework of the Kingdom of God and will recognise the need to reduce congregational activities to the essential minimum. This step may mean some radical restructuring of congregational activities. It is not a case of disbanding the congregation's role, as some would want, rather it is necessary to define its role more sharply.

vii. Identifies people's gifts and releases these within the congregation and/or local community

By viewing the congregation from the perspective of the Kingdom of God, congregational members will have to evaluate seriously their giftings and roles. For some, their calling and gifting will be primarily to minister within the fellowship. One such gifting is that of a pastor. Others may be involved in establishing and manning community activities and engaging in Kingdom warfare within the community. While others will be called into business, politics, to engage in trades, school teaching, or any of the numerous activities within the community. For church leaders to insist that such people be involved in more conventional areas of congregational life and to seek to lock them and their gifts up in the congregational structure is foolish. The role of the congregation is to support these people, pray for them and encourage them as they carry out the work to which God has called them.

God's desire is to see His will done in every area of society. A person working in the secular media, nursing, business or politics (as long as they do it according to the values of the Kingdom of God) can have just as significant a role in the Kingdom of God as the person who works in the church or church related community ministry.

We learned this principle when one of our elders was appointed to the position of principal in a large local High School. Both he and the other elders agreed that it was wrong for him to be tied down in leading the congregation. God had called him to a new task. In terms of the Kingdom of God this task was just as important as leading a congregation. He had to be released to God's call on his life. What was our new responsibility to him? To support, encourage and pray for him. Thus one of our leaders regularly meets with him in his office to pray with him in this responsibility that he has.

The work of such people, may not lead directly to growth in our congregation. But if people in the community are being forced to recognise evidences of the life and rule of the Kingdom of God, coming to faith in Christ and being established in that faith, (even if that means that they are attending other congregations) then that is all that matters! Such is a Kingdom view.

viii. Has a radical view of the role of money and possessions.

People involved in such a model of congregation life and activity will embrace a very different view about the role of possessions and money to that which much of the Church currently practises. They will realise that the principles of the Kingdom of God are often diametrically opposed to those of the society around them. They will be attempting to model such principles to the community around them. They will be committed to supporting each other with their financial and material resources. They will be reaching out to the poor in creative and effective ways and striving to release as much of their resources as possible for the work of the Kingdom of God.

ix. Assesses results in terms of the Kingdom of God

If we are to take seriously the Lord's command to 'seek first the Kingdom of God,' then we should be assessing the effectiveness of everything we do in the light of its impact for the Kingdom of God. We will have to learn to ask the following questions:

'Will this (does this/has this) activity of our congregation contributed to the overall advancement of the Kingdom of God?'

How can we enhance the effect of this ministry to more effectively demonstrate the Kingdom of God?'

'Are we spending a disproportionate amount of time on this activity and thus reducing opportunities for effective endeavours in other areas?'

All true ministry for Jesus is a witness to the Kingdom of God. To be part of a community of Christians seeking to explore the many avenues that result in working from a Kingdom framework, offers an exciting and rewarding experience.

The above suggestions bring together some of the things that the Holy Spirit has been saying to the Church over recent times. It is not an exhaustive list of all the features which should characterise a congregation. We have taken for granted that such areas as belief in the person and work of Christ, the necessity for prayer, the recognition of the inspiration of Scripture and other basic beliefs of our Christian faith would also be an essential part of any such model.

For some congregations to embrace such a model will mean quite substantial changes, particularly in their thinking and attitudes. For others it will mean reasonably small adjustments.

Our roots have given us a stucture which can embrace such features relatively easily. The priesthood of all believers encourages individuals to be accountable to the Lord and seek His direction in terms of worship and service. Our multiple leadership means that the load is spread across a group of people. With less emphasis on the ministry of ordained personnel, our structure is more that of networking rather than relying on hierarchical control and organisational methods. All of these factors have helped our congregation to move towards adapting to and accommodating such a model.

We will now seek to explore some of the practical ways in which such a model could function.

Community Ministries

Over the past ten or so years we have seen numerous groups form within the congregation who have sought to use gifts, skills, trades, and professions to minister to specific needs within the community. (Some of these are listed and explained in Appendix III). Initially this was not a strategy we decided upon. It has developed very much out of trial and error, with people being encouraged to seek creative ways by which they could impact the community and share the gospel with people.

We picture such community ministries as arrowheads (see Fig 5) which form contact points with the local community. These ministries are established from a support base within the congregation. The head of an arrow, by itself, is of very little effect, it also requires the shaft, the flights and a bow to achieve its function. Similarly those involved in a ministry within the community, unconnected to the congregation, will probably not be very effective. They will also require prayer support, finance and people resources.

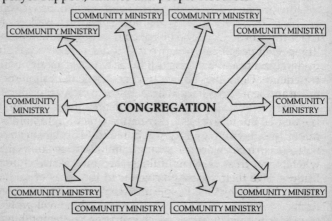

Figure 5. Model for congregational community ministries.

Operating principles for community ministries.
i. Autonomy

Congregational leadership has a special role to play in the formation of community ministries. These need to be given maximum autonomy. It is absolutely essential that congregational leadership does not seek to control such ministries. One of the most important qualities of leadership is the ability to release people. People must be freed to seek and sense God's call on their lives.

The responsibility of leadership is to determine before God the general direction in which the congregation should be moving. They must then provide for communication within the congregation, pastoral oversight of its people and for the equipping of its individuals. These are the areas of congregational life which leadership must own and take responsibility for.

Those in the congregation should be free to determine before God what it is He is calling them to be engaged in. People respond much better to their own God-given vision, than to one placed on them from others. It is essential that leaders take risks, trust people and are prepared to get their fingers burnt from time to time. People are people, tensions and problems will sometimes occur between those working together. Some will be strong in faith, others will be weaker. People go back on commitments, some may even walk away from the Lord. Occasionally a community ministry has 'flopped' or people have fallen out with each other because of disagreements and tensions. All these have been part of our experience. Obviously advice and encouragement should be given and sometimes it may be necessary to pick up the pieces and carry on when problems occur. A degree of accountability is essential but this needs to err on the side of light-handed rather than heavy-handed. Accountability is best nurtured within the framework of strong committed relationships where love, trust and truthfulness abound. Many church leaders have their greatest struggles in the areas of taking risks and releasing their people into what God is calling them to do. We tend to try to create situations which will protect against failure. In doing so, much initiative to attempt things for God may be taken away from people.

The story is told about Jesus arriving back in heaven after His work on earth and being met by the angel Gabriel. Gabriel is surprised that after the incredible lengths Jesus had gone to to redeem men and women, He should leave this message with such a group of weak, nondescript people. Jesus' reply was 'I have made no other arrangements.' Surely, this was 'risk *par excellence.*'

Very often the church leadership does not have the gifting or experience to direct or control a specific ministry to the community. I couldn't lead a pre-school music group and doubt whether any of our leadership could either! We have to trust people to do it and give them the right to try! Church leaders don't even have to plan it all. All they have to do is say, 'Dream some dreams, it's OK to have a go!'

In a sense these community ministries are 'para-church' in that they are visioned and birthed, not by the congregation as a whole but by individuals or groups within the congregation. The leadership then recognises these ministries, encourages others to become involved, communicates what is happening and seeks to offer pastoral and prayer support, and provide appropriate training, where necessary, to those involved.

ii. Adaptability

Another principle is that of maximum adaptability. Ministries will rise and fall. Social conditions will change, sometimes from year to year. People with certain skills will move on. It is unwise to seek to institutionalise community ministries and feel that once they are started they must be maintained for all time.

For several years we ran very successful unemployment programmes which catered for many young people in the area. However, staff moved on to other occupations and conditions changed, so we felt it wise to wind these up. All too often, congregations view the closing down of a ministry, an outreach or a congregational activity as a sign of defeat. Many are slavishly run, year after year, with suitable staff being obtained only by the arm twisting method!

iii. Economic component

When necessary, and where possible, an economic

component can be built into the ministry. It is important that ministries seek to be financially self-sufficient rather than being a constant drain on the congregation. A good rule is to attempt to make them high in people content and low in plant content. In our own case several ministries have formed their own trusts and raise finance in a variety of ways. Some charge for services rendered, others apply for Government finances or grants from community trusts.

In the past there has been something of a fear about mixing Christian ministry with making money! We were told that we cannot serve God and Mammon. This is, of course, true. However what we are talking about here is not the *serving* of mammon but the *using* of mammon. Very few Christian ministries get along without money!!

The creation and management of finance needs to be looked at very carefully and may require expertise beyond those who have the initial vision for the ministry. Those with skills in this area need to contribute and it is a good way to encourage others to become involved in a particular ministry. Such developments can lead to the establishment of teams of people working together and to the pooling of resources and expertise. Every congregation has entrepreneurs in its ranks. They are often sitting unfulfilled in the pew expending all their energies in making themselves wealthy. Leaders need to pray that such people will catch a vision of the Kingdom of God. May God give us more Spirit-filled entrepreneurs. May He then give us the ability to fire them with a vision of His Kingdom, the courage to release them into that ministry and then set a hedge about them so as they won't get ensnared by material prosperity themselves!

iv. Spiritual principles

To achieve maximum effectiveness, such ministries must operate in the same way as Jesus ministered while here on earth. Empowered by the Holy Spirit, motivated by the love of God, based on the precepts of Scripture and saturated with prayer. Human abilities alone can never extend the Kingdom of God.

v. Seek opportunities to pray with people

Often people in need are more ready for someone to pray with them than to be 'witnessed' to. I can not remember the last time that a person I have been seeking to help within our community has turned down my offer of prayer. I have prayed for people in car parks, offices, hospitals, homes, classrooms, street corners and even beaches. Prayer opens the opportunity for the Holy Spirit to do something that will attract the person's attention and cause them to think about spiritual things. Quite frequently the person prayed for has tears in their eyes by the end of the prayer. I well remember walking down the road one day and noticing a man trying to open the door of a woman's car. She had accidentally locked her keys inside. Coming back some thirty minutes later they were still struggling with the piece of wire seeking to raise the locking button. I watched for a moment or two and then offered to have a try. At that moment I sensed that God wanted me to pray aloud about this matter. Now, praying for people and praying for locked car doors are two quite different things! To my everlasting regret I ignored that conviction and prayed under my breath. I pushed the wire down beside the glass of the car window, jiggled it once or twice, pulled it up and instantly raised the locking button to the immense relief of the car's owner. I often wonder what would have been the woman's response if I had taken the opportunity to pray aloud!

vi. Networking with other community ministries

With various community ministries within our congregation (and other local congregations) considerable networking is possible. This enhances the contact that people from the local community have with Christians.

Levels of involvement

There are several levels of involvement within the community. Each has a valuable part to play and should be encouraged.

i. Personal level

People sometimes complain that their congregation or

their leadership is not interested in becoming involved within the community in the ways we have been describing. My response to this all too regular complaint, is to point out to the person that if God is calling them to a particular need in the community then they must obey Him. A Christian in a Citizen's Advice Bureau or on a playgroup committee can have a vital role in such an activity as an individual.

ii. *Family level*
A whole family can work together on a specific project. This offers marvellous opportunities for involving young people. It encourages them to reach out to human need and provides the opportunity for them to see God opening doors (and sometimes spiritual eyes!) through their involvement.

iii. *Small group level*
This would probably be the most frequent level of involvement. A group of people have a common vision and work together to achieve that vision. Such a ministry towards the community can give a house group a valuable outward looking vision.

iv. *Congregational level*
Some community ministries may need a much larger base of operation than just a small group. A congregation will have many skilled and gifted people and may be able to utilise such people in a strategic, combined, community ministry.

v. *Multi-congregational level*
Utilising the skills and abilities of people from several congregations in developing a specific community ministry, has its own problems as well as its own great advantages. The main advantage is that such a community ministry is not viewed with as much suspicion by those in the local area, as one run by a single congregation.

Great problems can be encountered if such a multi-congregational ministry has to be vetted by church boards or leadership before it can carry out any decisions. Here the principle of autonomy, mentioned above, comes into its own.

A group of Christians, coming from several congregations,

needs to be given the freedom to develop a ministry together without always having to return to the congregational leadership for permission to carry out its plans. It is sometimes difficult enough to get one group of church leaders to agree on a course of action, let alone several groups of church leaders! This area of co-operation between local churches offers a great opportunity to demonstrate to the world something of church unity (See Fig 6).

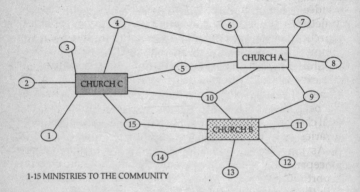

1-15 MINISTRIES TO THE COMMUNITY

Figure 6. Church unity through social concern.

What better way for a group of churches in a local community to demonstrate their oneness in Christ than for their members to roll up their sleeves and commit themselves to the compassionate service of their fellow human beings. For local congregations to co-operate together in this ministry of caring for people, rather than competing for the allegiance of people, would be a mighty testimony to a watching world.

It is unlikely that we will ever be able to demonstrate church unity, based around a common theology or a common ecclesiastical structure or common forms of worship. Even if we did, it is most unlikely that the watching world would be aware of such unity, let alone be impressed by it! But demonstrating unity by co-operating together to meet community needs – now that might just come to their attention. Such attempts are being made in various areas (See the story of Love Inc. 'Help is just around the Corner,' Virgil Gulker, Creation House, 1988.). The minimum level of theology required is that we seek to 'Love the Lord our God with all our heart and soul and strength and mind, and love our neighbour as ourself' (Luke 10:27). Surely we can agree on those two things!!

A good starting point for such co-operation would be for local congregations to list all the ministries they provide for the community. Unfortunately local congregations often have no idea what each other is doing and sadly, activities are sometimes unnecessarily duplicated. Not only do local churches not know what each other is doing but often the community doesn't know what is happening either.

Churches in our community have recently gone through this exercise and published in booklet form a list of the numerous services they offer to the community. This booklet has been distributed widely to schools, doctors' surgeries, local churches, welfare agencies, citizens advice centres, local libraries and Government departments.

As members of our congregation have explored these concepts we have seen a large number of effective and creative opportunities develop, which are reaching into the community with the love and power of God (See Appendix III).

Priorities of involvement

One of the dangers of community ministry is that those participating can become very involved and other areas of their life may suffer. The Bible is quite clear about what our order of priorities should be in our ministry to people.

i. Biological family must come first

Paul says to Timothy that 'if anybody does not provide for his relatives, and especially for his immediate family, he has denied the faith and is worse than an unbeliever' (1 Tim 5:8). To be so involved with the needs of others, but ignoring those of our own family is certainly not a reflection of the Kingdom of God. In fact, it is counter productive to the purposes of God.

ii. Church family comes next

We read in 1 John 3:17 that 'if anyone has material

possessions and sees his brother in need but has no pity on him, how can the love of God be in him?' Love between fellow members of the Body of Christ is a powerful testimony to a watching world and must take priority over our concern for those outside our congregation.

iii. World family comes last

In Galatians 6:10 we read, 'Therefore, as we have opportunity, let us do good to all people, especially to those who belong to the family of God.' Here we have a clearly defined priority. Good to all – but especially to those of the family of God.

It is not a case of perfectly caring for the needs of biological family before we can help those in our fellowship or in the community. We will probably never be able to completely and perfectly care for people at any level. It seems to be more a case of emphasis. At certain times of our lives, our biological family has greater needs than at others, such needs must be attended to first. Within a congregation some people can become involved in caring for the special needs of those in their fellowship thus freeing others to minister to the community. Whatever the case, God's order of priority must be observed.

How to start ministries to the community
Congregations need to ask the following questions.

i. What are the needs in our community?

To answer such a question may mean some research into the local community. In Biblical terms this is 'looking at the fields' (John 4:35).

ii. What are the resources that we have available?

There will always be more needs than there are resources to meet them. We can not hope to meet all needs and should not be upset that we can't.

iii. Is this what God wants us to do?

Good ideas are never enough to demonstrate and establish the Kingdom of God. People must know the call and direction of God on their lives if they are going to continue in an activity geared to meeting needs within the community, and if this is going to see fruit for the Kingdom of God. When the going gets tough it's important to know that God has called one into this ministry.

iv. Does God want us to do this now?

We have found that the timing of the commencement of a ministry may be as important as ascertaining what the particular ministry should be. In the instance of the shop and the Family Care Centre (see Appendix III), God gave the vision of these several years before they were birthed. The period between seeing the possibility and birthing the ministry was crucial. It enabled the vision to be prayed through and focused more sharply.

Individual Christians need to be asking themselves the following questions:

What abilities, gifts, or skills has God given me? How can I best use these for the glory of God and to demonstrate His Kingdom?

Is my calling and gifting primarily towards the congregation or the community?

Can I pool my resources with others to minister to people's needs?

How can I model something of the Kingdom of God to those around me?

Church leaders will need to help people in their congregations discover answers for these questions and then encourage opportunities to be taken to utilise people's gifts and abilities.

Conclusion

In conclusion, we see that this model of the church theologically embraces –

The Kingdom of God
The ministry of the Spirit
Social concern

Evangelism
Ministry to the poor
Loving our neighbour
Servanthood
Unity between Christians
Team ministry.

Using the analogy of an army, a congregation should be seen as the base camp of an army at war. Here the soldiers are equipped, encouraged, supported, provided for and then thrust into the front lines for combat with the enemy. At the camp principles are established, planning is carried out, structures are created and strategies are devised. These are communicated to those involved in the conflict and then they are encouraged to get on with the battle. Obviously there needs to be a close link between the camp and the front lines. Those on the front lines fight the battle according to guidelines laid down by those in command at the base camp. However, they are permitted considerable flexibility when it comes to engaging the enemy. The army camp does not exist for itself, it's there to support those at the front and help them win the battle. Some people have a greater role at the camp, others on the front line, but all are striving to the one end – the winning of the war; in terms of what we are saying – the seeking of God's Kingdom. In the front lines, where the battle is the most intense, it doesn't matter very much if you're black or white, educated or uneducated, rich or poor, Baptist or Methodist – everyone is striving together towards the common goal, that of defeating the enemy. This enemy is Satan and the inroads he has made into human lives and society, it is not the people around us.

Too often our congregations have had a fortress mentality – seeking to protect the Lord's people from the evil influence of the world around. Instead of seeing our roles as 'salt' and 'light' and encouraging people to penetrate all areas of our communities. We have been too defensively minded.

We need to encourage people to demonstrate an alternative lifestyle to those around about and seek to bring the rule of God into every area in which we have influence. As we do this we see the principles of the Kingdom of God established and men and women coming out of the kingdom of darkness and into the Kingdom of His Son.

The Future

In the light of all we have been saying what does the future hold?

Scripture clearly indicates that things toward the end of the age will get worse and worse. We read of 'distress in nations, men's hearts failing them for fear' (Lk 2:25-26), `perilous times' (2 Tim 3:1) and `seducing spirits' (1 Tim 4:1). In one of His Kingdom parables, Jesus made it clear that wheat and tares would be growing together until the end of the world (Matt 13:24-30, 37-43). Tares are the sons of the evil one, while wheat represents the sons of the Kingdom of God. Both will be present at the end of the age. Obviously the Kingdom of God will not overcome all evil prior to the Lord's return.

Some have taken these passages to indicate that there is not much that the followers of Christ can do about all this. It will be all gloom and doom until the return of Christ. Such a view says, 'The best we can hope to do is rescue men and women from the storm.'

Certainly the Church must be committed to rescuing people from the kingdom of darkness and seeing them established in the Kingdom of God but, as we have sought to point out in this book, there is more to the gospel than just the 'salvation of souls.' As the influence of the kingdom of darkness increases around this planet, so will opportunities for the influence of the Kingdom of God.

In a nutshell the vision that God seems to be growing in many groups of His people is that He wants to establish a visible evidence of His Kingdom in their community.

Teams of Holy Spirit-filled and led people, co-operating in close, committed relationships, will use their skills, talents and gifts to meet the needs of the community in a wholistic way. Members of congregations will simplify their lifestyles in order to free up finance for the establishment of Christian enterprises to cater for the growing pressures and needs of people in our societies. As Governments struggle to meet budgets and cut back on social welfare spending, Christians will be the first to volunteer their services and finances to serve and love those in need. Rehabilitation and contact centres will be established and manned by Christians who are filled with the Holy Spirit. As they reach out to meet the needs of a disintegrating society, they will form bridgeheads for the gospel and will find unprecedented opportunities to share the Good News. God will change lives, minister to deep needs through His people, and bring many into His Kingdom.

Those around us will want to know how these changes are happening in the lives of people and what the principles are upon which we operate. We will be able to point out to them that we are unashamedly Christian, that we build all we do on Biblical principles and prayer, and seek to love people as Jesus would have. In turn local groups and Government agencies will be prepared to send people with disturbed backgrounds, from prison sentences, with drug backgrounds and family distress, to the various agencies that God is raising up.

In the face of the decline in family life, drug abuse, violence, alcoholism, economic problems, sexual promiscuity and perversion, race and ethnic tensions what is to be the response of the Christian Church? God seems to be saying to His people –

'Don't curse the darkness, light candles!! Model the lifestyle of My Kingdom. Demonstrate a viable alternative. Be a city set upon a hill. Penetrate your local community and be the salt I mean you to be.'

We have a long way to go. As fellowships of Christians we are only scratching the surface of the potential we have within our congregations. We are slow to learn and slower to change. We are unaccustomed to cost and sacrificial commitment.

Do we dare to permit the living God to walk among us, transforming our attitudes, motives and actions, quickening vision and rekindling in us a passionate love for Him and His purposes? If we were to, maybe we would have the privilege of seeing scores of people coming to faith in Christ. Sometimes this would be as a direct result of our participation in their needs and sometimes as a combination of factors such as friendship, 'power events', ministering to need and preaching.

Is it not just conceivable, that we have within our grasp, the possibility of drawing the attention of whole communities, maybe even whole nations, to the reality of the Kingdom of God and the claims of Jesus Christ?

APPENDIX I

KINGDOM MANIFESTO

Preamble

It is with growing conviction and excitement that we present to you this Kingdom Manifesto – a statement concerning the Kingdom of God which is the rule and government of God over all of life, individual and corporate, private and public.

In many places in Aotearoa, New Zealand, there is an increasing interest and awakening to the realisation that when Jesus Christ the Son of God commanded His disciples to pray *'Your Kingdom Come'* and to *'Seek first the Kingdom of God'* in everyday matters, He expected it to have a profound motivating effect on His followers of that day and down through the ages.

Many churches in the 20th century have not yet fully discovered the dynamic of these commands. But in this country and overseas, Christians are enthusiastically exploring, studying and allowing the Holy Spirit to lead them into fresh understanding about the Kingdom of God. Clearly the Kingdom of God was the central theme in the teachings of Jesus. It is much more radical than most Christians have conceived. We believe that the Christian community needs to recapture and apply the importance of this message.

This statement does not include all the issues that encompass an understanding of the Kingdom of God but we believe that it covers some of those that are of greatest significance in our country at this time.

We believe that the content of this statement encompasses views held by Church orthodoxy through the 2000 years of its history and that throughout the entire Church age, eschatological liberty has generally been granted to others in the Body of Christ so that neither premillenialism, amillenialism or postmillenialism has been considered a heresy by the mainstream theologians of the Church.

We present this Manifesto to you as a vision of the possibilities of a wholehearted commitment to the Kingdom of God by the people of God in Aotearoa, New Zealand.

We confess that all too often:

* We have ignored the centrality of the message of the Kingdom of God in the teaching of Jesus
* We have failed to recognise that love is the definitive mark of the Kingdom of God – loving the Lord our God with all our heart, soul, strength and mind and our neighbours as ourselves
* We have limited the expression of Christ's Kingdom within society to the institutional church
* We have emphasised the individual and personal aspects of the Kingdom of God to the neglect of the corporate and communal
* We have neglected the physical and material implications of the Kingdom of God and concentrated on the moral and the spiritual
* We have divided our lives and activities into secular and sacred categories
* We have failed to occupy our proper position as servants in the affairs of Government, education, business, economics, trade unions, media, arts, science, welfare and medicine as the Creator's salt and light to the world so that those areas of life might more clearly reflect Christ's justice, hope, peace and joy
* We have prayed *'Your Kingdom Come'* and ignored the command of Christ to *'Seek it first'* in our personal and societal lifestyles

Therefore we repent of our failure to let Christ be King in these areas. We will redress these failures with teaching, small group discovery, seeking new insights, creative Spirit-led endeavour, robust theological debate and the development of working models embodying principles of the Kingdom of God.

To this end we offer this KINGDOM MANIFESTO as a call to new obedience to our Lord Jesus Christ.

1. Biblical Base

'The Lord is a great God and King above all gods'. As the Creator, Sustainer, Owner and Controller of the whole universe He has never given up, nor will He ever give up, His rule over this universe.

In the Biblical record from **Old Testament** times, we see God creating the world and placing it under the management and authority of women and men – both created in the image of God[1]. Subsequently men and women disobeyed their creator and this rebellion has influenced and spoiled the whole of God's creation[2]. Yet God still desired to establish His authority and rule in the lives of individual people and in the nation of Israel. Through many of the experiences of His chosen people and the statements made by the prophets, God taught them to once again expect His actual rule on earth. This new era would ultimately affect the whole world, bringing salvation, justice, and peace – wholeness in all areas of life – to men and women[3].

In the **New Testament** we see that Jesus Christ, the son of David and the Son of God, came to earth to commence this promised age by proclaiming and demonstrating the Kingdom of God[4]. His life attracted women, men and children from all walks of life. Young and old, rich and poor, educated and uneducated, religious and non-religious, Greeks, Romans and Jews were all astonished at His gracious words and His powerful works. These evidences, coupled with the climax to His life – His death, resurrection and return to the Father – unmistakably proclaimed the present reality of the reign of God on earth.

But Jesus' understanding of the Kingdom differed from that which had been expected. The Kingdom of God had not fully come with His presence on earth but was a hidden, apparently insignificant, yet steadily growing influence[5]. Nor was it merely a political kingdom – Jesus firmly rejected the use of violence and the use of military power as a means for its establishment[6]. He re-defined the enemy of God's Kingdom as Satan, with his evil forces, and all people who join him in opposing God. Through His works of power, culminating in His resurrection, He demonstrated the victory of the Kingdom of God over the enemy and guaranteed the final triumph over death and all evil[7]. However the battle still continues today and will do so until the return of Christ. Although Christians debate the details of that return, it will usher in the Kingdom of God in all its fullness.

Meanwhile, Jesus has sent the Holy Spirit to equip, enable and empower men and women to see, proclaim and demonstrate the Good News of the Kingdom of God to this world[8]. Understanding the importance of the Kingdom of God and of the death and resurrection of Jesus Christ, the writers of the New Testament explained that the Kingdom of God requires Jesus to be honoured as Lord and Master over every aspect of life[9]. Since that time the message of the Kingdom of God has proved to be relevant and effective worldwide. Christ the King transcends all racial, national, sexual, educational, cultural, socio-economic and religious barriers. The presence of the Kingdom of God through the power of the Holy Spirit here and now, and the knowledge of its climax at Christ's return is Good News indeed for each generation[10].

2. The King and His Kingdom

2.1 **We believe** that Jesus Christ is the King of His Kingdom[11]. Therefore He is our central focus and we seek to worship, love, obey and follow Him in our walk in the Kingdom of God.

2.2 **We believe** that the Kingdom of God is evident on earth when the will of God is being done[12]. It is the expression of the life of God in His people corporately. It is the rule of God in the lives of women and men.

Therefore we encourage all women, men and children to commit themselves to that Kingdom by placing themselves under the rule of Jesus Christ and acknowledging Him as Lord of their lives.

2.3 **We believe** that it was God, through His Spirit, who enabled Jesus to proclaim and demonstrate the Kingdom of God while He was on earth[13].

Therefore we encourage women and men to seek the gifts

of Holy Spirit and know the Holy Spirit's empowering as they 'seek first the Kingdom of God'.

2.4 **We believe** that the basis for our understanding of God's Kingdom is found in Jesus (the revelation of God to people) and the Bible, God's record of that revelation[14].
Therefore we fully acknowledge the trustworthiness of Scripture and seek to interpret all matters of faith and conduct in the light of its teaching under the guidance of the Holy Spirit.

3. Signs of the Kingdom of God

We believe that the following are significant signs of the presence of the Kingdom of God –

3.1 The presence of Jesus in the midst of His gathered people[15].
Therefore we look to the Church to be both a sign of and a signpost to the Kingdom of God as we experience the joy, peace and sense of celebration which His presence brings.

3.2 The proclamation of the Gospel[16].
Therefore, as Jesus communicated the gospel we will also seek to do this by all means, in all places, at all times and encourage all followers of Jesus to do likewise.

3.3 Conversion and the new birth[17].
Therefore we will expect to see the Holy Spirit bringing people out of the Kingdom of darkness and into the Kingdom of God.

3.4 Deliverance from the forces of evil[18]. We take seriously the power of evil in the affairs of men and women; through people's personal behaviour, in the Godlessness seen in every culture, and the occult practices within our society.
Therefore we will minister in the name of Jesus to all who are under the influence of the devil and will challenge the faulty teachings and worldviews that tend to dominate the minds of women and men today.

3.5 The Holy Spirit working in power[19]. We expect to see God transforming people and performing miracles and healings today.
Therefore we will seek to be willing vessels through whom the Holy Spirit can bring such evidences that the Kingdom of God is amongst us.

3.6 The fruit of the Holy Spirit in the lives of people[20].

Therefore we wait patiently to see the qualities that mark the life of Jesus being expressed in the lives of His followers. We earnestly desire that our personal lives also demonstrate such qualities.

3.7 Suffering for righteousness sake[21]. We live in a period of incomplete realisation of the Kingdom of God, in a state of tension. A courageous joyous bearing of suffering is a clear sign to onlookers that we are part of God's Kingdom.

Therefore, as Jesus suffered, we will not be surprised if suffering comes to us.

4. Entering the Kingdom of God

4.1 **We believe** that a person enters the Kingdom of God by repentance and faith in Jesus Christ the Lord, being born again by the work of the Spirit of God on the basis of the death and resurrection of Jesus[22].

Therefore we do all in our power to urge people to enter that Kingdom where women and men of all races are equal.

4.2 **We believe** that while the Kingdom of God is open to all people, Jesus declared a particular concern for the poor, weak, and oppressed, and He said that it may be more difficult for the powerful, the wealthy or the influential of this world to enter it[23].

Therefore we are committed to reflecting Jesus' concern as we proclaim the Good news of the Kingdom of God.

5. The Kingdom of God and the Church

5.1 **We believe** that the Church is the community of the King, the Body of Christ, a visible evidence of His presence and God's chosen agent to demonstrate His Kingdom in this world[24].

Therefore we will work for its continuing renewal and seek the total mobilisation of all its members to be salt and light in their local communities.

5.2 **We believe** that at the local level the Church is the people of God sharing together in loving worship, fellowship, nurture and training for ministry in the world[25].

Therefore, in our congregations, we will strive for

maximum effectiveness in these areas, and encourage Christians to identify, develop and use their gifts in order to demonstrate the Kingdom of God in all areas of society.

5.3 **We believe** the Church transcends all denominational differences, and is made up of women and men from all nations, cultures, ages and walks of life who are being transformed by the power of the Spirit of God[26].

Therefore, the worship and life of each local congregation should affirm the heritage of each culture represented in its midst, allowing this diversity to enrich and enhance our service of God.

5.4 **We believe** that Church growth is the normal outcome of seeking first the Kingdom of God[27].

Therefore, where Christians do this, local congregations will grow and new congregations will be planted and established.

5.5 **We believe** that a loving, servant heart towards God and other people is the prime characteristic of being 'Kingdom people'[28].

Therefore we seek to demonstrate this in our congregations, communities and all other areas of life.

5.6 **We believe** that the Church does not exist for itself but was established by Christ as a witness to the Kingdom of God[29].

Therefore, in our local congregations, we will set goals and evaluate their effectiveness in terms of that Kingdom.

6. Opposition to the Kingdom of God

6.1 **We believe** that the schemes of Satan oppose the Kingdom of God and that there is continual and hostile conflict between the Kingdom of God and the Kingdom of Satan[30].

Therefore we expect opposition to the establishment of the Kingdom of God in our own lives, in our families, in our communities and in our country.

6.2 **We believe** that through the death and resurrection of Jesus Christ, the Kingdom of God demonstrates the power which will ultimately overcome all sin, poverty, disease, death and demonic interference[31].

Therefore we declare, and seek to live in the triumph of the Kingdom of God over the powers of darkness.

7. The Kingdom of God and Human Relationships

7.1 **We believe** that an understanding of the Kingdom of God will bring men and women to a deeper appreciation of the peace and justice of God[32].

Therefore we determine to act justly, oppose all forms of violence and be resolutely involved in seeking peace and justice in every situation as and when we are able.

7.2 **We believe** that reconciliation is at the heart of the message of the gospel of the Kingdom and is firstly between God and people then between people themselves[33].

Therefore we place great importance on reconciliation among and between different nations, cultures, local communities, churches and families.

7.3 **We believe** the Kingdom of God encourages caring and sharing lifestyles as opposed to materialism and individualism[34].

Therefore we urge cooperation rather than competition, and oppose the consumerism and materialism of much of Western society. We are personally committed to living a sacrificial and simpler lifestyle.

7.4 **We believe** that God instituted marriage and family life as the fundamental unit for expressing the life of the Kingdom in society. The rule of Christ brings dignity and sanctity to both the single and married states[35].

Therefore we will model and support fidelity within a permanent marriage covenant between one man and one woman, and chastity outside of marriage.

7.5 **We believe** that God delegates authority to women and men within His Kingdom, raises up leaders and expects those in such positions to act responsibly and with humility[36].

Therefore we encourage those in authority within the Kingdom of God to model servant leadership, act with integrity, seek accountability and encourage teamwork.

8. The Kingdom of God and Society

8.1 **We believe** that the proclamation of the Gospel of the Kingdom requires identification with the needs of those to whom we speak[37].

Therefore we are committed to ministering to the whole person and reject the distinction which would isolate evangelism from social involvement.

8.2 **We believe** that God's intention is the transformation of the whole of society and this transformation is inseparable from the transformation of the inner, spiritual life of people, families and communities[38].

Therefore we encourage men and women to look to God Himself for the power for this transformation.

8.3 **We believe** that God is the rightful owner of this universe, but He has given the management of this planet to men and women[39].

Therefore we are committed to a wise and responsible stewardship of land and other natural resources and we are opposed to all forms of greed or exploitation.

8.4 **We believe** that the Kingdom of God affects the whole of a person's being[40].

Therefore we are concerned about physical, cultural, social, spiritual, intellectual and emotional wholeness in human lives.

8.5 **We believe** that the Kingdom of God addresses all the needs that women and men experience[41].

Therefore we are concerned to minister to the needs of – the rich and the poor, the imprisoned and the free, the oppressor and the oppressed, the over-fed and the hungry. As well as all others in need.

8.6 **We believe** we must respond to all people in need, especially sisters and brothers in the Kingdom of God[42].

Therefore we will give from our material abundance to assist the economic and spiritual transformation of the lives of people in poverty in other parts of the world.

8.7 **We believe** that the Kingdom of God transcends and transforms all cultures. It is radically different from, and challenges the fallenness of the status quo in our communities[43].

Therefore, while recognising the contribution, strengths and uniqueness of each culture within our multicultural society, we are committed to bringing the influence of the Kingdom of God to bear on the fallen structures in our society by modelling the alternative and distinctive lifestyle of the Kingdom of God.

8.8 **We believe** that whenever humans, individuals or societies, Christian or non-Christian, generally obey the moral, economic, and practical precepts of the Kingdom of God, those people tend to reap earthly blessings for doing that[44].

Therefore we recognise the common grace of God to all people.

9. The Kingdom of God and the Future

9.1 **We believe** that Jesus Christ will return and that it is God the Father's intention to reconcile all things to Himself through Christ[45].

Therefore we wait expectantly for the time when the full reign of the Kingdom of God will be seen and the whole of creation will be healed and restored.

9.2 **We believe** that the Kingdom of God is both a present reality and a future expectation. It is both 'already' and 'not yet fully'. We live in the period between the inauguration and consummation of the Kingdom. At that consummation all the kingdoms of this world will come under the reign of Christ[46].

Therefore we seek its demonstration here on earth while awaiting its full revelation in the future.

9.3 **We believe** that there is an important role for this earth in the future under the rule and reign of Jesus Christ the King[47].

Therefore we will value not only the spiritual but also the material and physical elements of creation as we work with Christ for the redemption of things.

10. Commitment to the Kingdom of God

10.1 **We believe** that commitment to the cause of the Kingdom of God will mean costly discipleship for people in terms of time, possessions, money and abilities[48].

Therefore we will stress to people the need for prayerful evaluation of their life's priorities, discipline and faithfulness.

10.2 **We believe** that people were created to live within the Kingdom of God and that they thrive under its rule[49].

Therefore, it is living by the principles of the Kingdom of God that people reach their maximum potential and experience life in all its fullness. Thus the Kingdom of God is not a threat to humanity.

10.3 **We believe** that the Kingdom of God calls us to develop our abilities to their fullest potential for God[50].

Therefore we will encourage people to pray for and pursue this by training, development and persistence in the vocational, sporting, creative, educational and relationship activities of their lives.

10.4 **We believe** the Kingdom of God is like a treasure hid in a field, a pearl of great price[51].

Therefore we will value everything we possess in relation to the Kingdom of God.

Final Summation

As Christians of Aotearoa, New Zealand, **we believe** the Kingdom call of God requires that we observe His Kingly rule

- **in all things.**
  Therefore there is no human activity, no region of human endeavour which is beyond His reign.
- **at all times.**
  Therefore we maintain that there is no distinction between the sacred and the secular areas of human life.
- **in all places.**
  Therefore we urge all Christians to 'seek first the Kingdom of God' in the home, at work, in study, in their local community, during recreation and in all other activities of their lives.
- **among all people.**
  Therefore we will work for racial and social harmony, international justice and peace, and the manifestation of His Kingdom among all people everywhere.
- **as our highest priority in our lives.**
  Therefore we will not permit anything to deflect us from seeking its fulfilment in our lives.

It is **therefore** our determined and unanimous decision, with prayer and the Holy Spirit's enabling, to commit ourselves to the outworking of this Manifesto. It is also our prayer that all who read this statement will join us in this commitment.

Ma te Atua Koe e arahi i nga wa katoa; (God lead you on).

REFERENCES

1. Genesis 1:27-28
    Galatians 3:28
2. Genesis 3
3. Isaiah 9:6-7
    Isaiah 65:17-25
4. Matthew 9:35
    Matthew 4:17-24
5. Matthew 13:31-33
6. John 18:36
7. Hebrews 2:14-15
8. John 14:16-18
    Acts 1:8
9. Philippians 3:7-8
10. Revelation 11:15
11. Philippians 2:9-11
12. Matthew 6:10
13. Luke 4:18-19
14. John 14:9-11
15. Colossians 1:18
16. Mark 1:15
17. John 3:3,5
18. Ephesians 6:10-18
    Colossians 2:1-3
    Matthew 12:28
19. 1 Corinthians 12:4-11
20. Galatians 5:19-26
21. 1 Peter 4:12-16
22. John 3:3,5
    Acts 2:38
    Romans 1:17
23. 1Corinthians 1:26-31
    Matthew 19:24
24. Ephesians 1:22-23
    Ephesians 3:10

27. Matthew 16:18-19
28. Luke 10:25-37
    Matthew 20:25-28
29. Matthew 16:18-19
30. Matthew 12:28
    Colossians 1:12-13
31. Colossians 2:15
32. Micah 6:8
    Romans 14:17
33. Colossians 1:20
34 John 13:34-35
35 Matthew 19:4-6
36. Hebrews 13:17
    1 Timothy 3
37. Mark 16:15
    Matthew 25:31-46
38. Colossians 1:10-22
39. Psalm 24:1
    Genesis 1:28
40. 1 Thessalonians 5:23
41. James 2:15-17
    1 John 3:16-17
    Galatians 6:10
42. Luke 4:18-19
    James 2:5
    Galatians 6:10
43. Galatians 3:28
44. Prov 11:24-27
45. John 14:3
    Colossians 1:19
46. Luke 17:21
    Luke 19:11
47. Zechariah 14:9
    Psalm 2:8

25. Acts 2:42-47
    1 Corinthians 12
    Ephesians 4:7-11
    Romans 12:4-8
26. Colossians 3:11
    Ephesians 2:11-19

    Colossians 1:18-20
48. Matthew 13:44
    Luke 18:22-30
    Luke 14:25-33
49. Matthew 6:25-34
50. Colossians 3:17
51. Matthew 13:45-46

Compiled by – Wyn Fountain, Brian Hathaway, Gordon Miller, Bernie Ogilvy, Peter Philip and Ray Windsor, after deliberation with other Evangelical and Charismatic Church leaders in New Zealand and overseas.

APPENDIX II

WE HAVE A VISION

We have a vision of a people who recognize:

That Jesus Christ is Lord. They know everything comes from Him and should be used for Him.

That this life is temporary – a springboard for future responsibilities and service, and they are stewards of their possessions, abilities, money and time.

That it is the Holy Spirit who empowers and motivates people to Kingdom living. It is He who transforms sinners, gives gifts to God's people and causes a transformation in the economic relationships between the people of God.

That the Church as the Body of Christ is a new society. A community dependent on God and each other for all spiritual and material needs. Who enjoy the depth and reality of genuine koinonia.

We have a vision of a people:

Who enjoy the security of deep committed relationships with each other.

Who, when – one suffers all suffer
– one rejoices all rejoice
– one experiences economic trouble others meet that need
– one falls into sin others restore that one.

Who base their relationships on co-operation rather than competition.

Who are available to each other, liable for each other and accountable to each other.

Who are filled with the spirit of servanthood towards their brothers and sisters in Christ and their local community.

About whom the world is forced to exclaim – 'See how these Christians love each other – and us.'

We have a vision of a people who recognize the strength of team ministry:

We see professional people, trades and business people using skills interdependently to bless the people of God and their surrounding communities.

We see musicians, crafts people and artists employing their creative talents in the pursuit of excellence to the glory of God.

We see the Holy Spirit being pleased to bless teams of people in healing, counselling and service ministries.

We have a vision of a people:

Who know God blesses them so they can bless others.

Whose lives are rivers of joyful giving rather than reservoirs of selfish greed.

Who live by Kingdom principles and know Kingdom security.

Whose pleasures are not dependent on the intrigue of the latest 'new gimmick' but on the everyday pleasures available from the hand of their Maker.

Who are infected with a joyous simplicity in all they do.

We have a vision of a people:

Who have voluntarily assumed a standard of living below (sometimes well below) what their income could allow.

Who are free from the pressure of having to buy bigger and better or from getting more and more.

Whose finance is invested in projects for the Kingdom of God, rather than in the kingdom of darkness. In business generating finance for the Kingdom of God.

Who are committed to living with less in order that they might share more.

We have a vision of a people:

Who seek to reach out to the poor in creative and productive ways.

Who seek to correct the causes of poverty as well as release the poor from their immediate need.

Who hear, and feel for, the suffering of those in the third world, seeking to meet those needs according to their resources and expertise.

We have a vision of a community whose lifestyle is:

So radically contradictory to the world's ways and thinking,

Such a prophetic condemnation to its values,

Such a contrast to its way of living that it may bring them into rejection and trouble with some areas of society,

but will also bring immeasurable glory and praise to their Lord Whom they love and serve.

WE HAVE A VISION.

Te Atatu Bible Chapel Leaders
August 1986.

APPENDIX III

COMMUNITY INVOLVEMENT

Below is a list of some of the major involvements that people attending Te Atatu Bible Chapel have had during the 1980's. Some have existed for a limited period of time, many exist at the time of writing.

Some of these activities involve people from other local congregations, while others are 'para-church' activities which people in the congregation are encouraged to participate in.

Such a variety of activities enables considerable 'networking' to occur and this provides opportunity for further support to those ministering in specific areas.

It is not recommended that people use this as a resource of good ideas to try. Needs in different communities vary, as do people's interests and gifts in local congregations.

* *Adventure Specialities*

Adventure Specialities recognises that the wilderness is a unique environment that God has historically used to build character in groups and individuals – such qualities as leadership skills, self-discipline, problem solving, stress management, group dynamics, contemplation and trust upon Him.

By providing and promoting excellence in top quality equipment and expertise, the staff and volunteers, tailor-make wilderness trips running combinations of kayaking (sea & white-water), rafting, rock and mountain climbing, tramping, camping, snow courses, caving, abseiling and other outdoor activities.

A wide range of groups benefit from this eg. Probation Service, Social Welfare, schools, unemployment programmes, youth groups, companies and Birthright.

An associated Adventure Club promotes further contact running regular meetings and trips away. Father and son courses are also run.

* *Between the Banks Shop*

The main aim of this shop is to be a Christian witness in the shopping centre.It also provides an outlet for crafts people to sell crafts and provides a range of Christian books to the public. It seeks to be a place of love and peace, where people can be encouraged, counselled and prayed for. Profits from trading are returned to worthwhile causes within the community.

* *Between the Banks Trust*

This trust was set up by Te Atatu Bible Chapel to provide for ministry to the community. Several areas of community involvement come under this trust and the trustees are members of the congegation. All of the money generated by (or given to) the trust is used within the community – none is used by the churches. Loans and gifts are made from this trust to worthwhile community activities.

* *Budgeting*

To help those under financial stress to get a better understanding of basic money management by giving advice and help in these areas. People are referred to this service through community workers and from Government Departments and community help agencies. A trained budget advisor works with the person seeking to sort out the financial situation.

* *Christian Books Supplied to Local Libraries*

In cooperation with other local churches Between the Banks Shop subsidised a selection of good Christian books which were placed free of charge in local libraries. Books selected included true life stories and books on family relationships.

* *Christmas Dinner for Lonely People*

For many people Christmas day can be very lonely and

sad with nobody with which to share it. Some members of the congregation have invited one or two strangers into their home who have been in such a position on Christmas day. This venture has been advertised through local radio stations.

* *Community Newspaper*
    A Christian community newspaper was run for a while. This included articles of interest from the local community, publicity of upcoming church events, testimonies and other matters of local interest.

* *Community Vegetable Garden*
    A project involving unemployed young people who grew a variety of vegetables. These were either sold at reduced prices or given away and distributed to local needy families.

* *Community Family Parties*
    Several wholesome family parties have been run. Here the whole family is catered for. Especially valuable around the Christmas period.

* *Co-operative House Building Ventures*
    Professional and trades people cooperating to get young families into their first homes.

* *Coaching for Examinations*
    With many High School teachers in the congregation, opportunities have been given for young people from the surrounding community to receive extra tuition. This has particularly involved those sitting senior examinations.

* *Emergency Housing*
    We provide accommodation to people in desperate need of housing and seek to minister to these people while they are in the home.
    There are several emergency homes available. One is a self-contained 2 bedroomed unit where 24 hour care, including meals and washing, is offered for short terms of 6-8 days for those in crisis situations. Others are available for longer term accommodation needs (up to 16 weeks) while people are

seeking a more permanent residence.

* Family Care Centre. Medical/Counselling Centre

The Family Care centre has been established to be a specifically Christian medical practice with a commitment to whole-person ministry. Health and wholeness implies reconciliation with God. The personnel involved are all Christians and seek to demonstrate and commend the gospel in both word and deed.

The Centre provides the services of a general practitioner with interest in the medical needs of young families. A woman doctor works part time. A professionally trained and experienced Christian counsellor is available for personal, marriage and family counselling. Selected Christian people with specific gifts are used where appropriate for specific needs. eg 'ministry of inner healing'.

A Christian lawyer attends by appointment.

As the Centre expands it is hoped to provide educational seminars in areas such as Antenatal, Parenting, Grief, Marriage Preparation and Enrichment. These would utilise Christian people with appropriate gifts and skills.

* Financial Aid

Financial aid is provided in the form of loans, interest free, to people who require it. Such aid covers bridging finance for homes and funds for those heavily in debt and having to pay high commercial interest rates. Each case is judged on its merits and those who have got into financial problems through unwise activities must agree to some budgeting help before the loan is given.

* Food Bank

This was run as a branch operation from a larger food bank and provided food at cheaper costs for selected families.

* Full-time Community Workers

These people seek to bring the love and power of God to people in the local community by meeting the needs of people – body, soul and spirit. They also network with other local Christian groups who have a vision for the local community.

Physical work such as lawns, cutting hedges, housework is carried out for those in need. Also transport for doctors visits, help to find accommodation and liaison with Government Departments.

Spiritual support is also provided through Christian love, prayer, counsel and the opportunity for the Holy Spirit to minister through His gifts.

* Holiday Films
Catering for children and provides relief for stressed mothers during vacation times.

* Industrial Chaplaincy
Chaplains seek to offer help and Christian guidance to those in the workplace who have personal, family or work related difficulties. They also seek to encourage practising Christians in the workplace and demonstrate to non-Christians the value of a Christian faith by encouraging them to think about spiritual issues. In representing the church in the workplace they can seek to communicate back to the church some of the social realities they encounter.

* Local Politics
From time to time people in the congregation have felt that they should stand for positions in the local government. This has been encouraged and supported. Sometimes finance has been made available from Between the Banks Trust.

* Marriage Counselling
Set up to assist engaged couples to understand the Biblical view of marriage so that they have a firm base for starting married life. Also seeks to assist married couples who are having difficulties in their marriage to acquire skills/ techniques to overcome their problems and to understand the situation from a Biblical point of view.

Use is made of questionnaires, and handout sheets to pinpoint the problem. Biblical guidelines are given on such areas as communication, role of husband/wife, conflict resolution, finances, self esteem. Homework of a specific nature is given and checked the following week.

Encouragement of couples is given by listening, giving counsel, praying and supporting.

* Ministry to Homosexuals

Is a transdenominational ministry set up to promote hope, growth and healing in homosexual men and women, their loved ones and friends.

Also seeks to bring knowledge and understanding of homosexuality to all Christians so as to enable them to reach out for help.

Face to face counselling is provided as well as a 24 hour Answerphone service. Support groups for homosexual men and women operate and also groups for spouses or parents affected by the homosexuality of a loved one. Educational resources such as printed materials, audio and video tapes and speakers are available, as is further information for those who desire to uphold the work of Exodus by prayer or financial support.

* Multi Purpose Church Building

When the congregation needed a new building it was decided to build a multi-purpose building rather than a sanctuary. This means local community groups can make more use of it.

* Open Homes Foundation

Seeks to bring the love and healing of Jesus Christ to families who are in need, especially where there is child abuse, neglect or where there are relationship and behaviour problems. Believes that a stable home, rather than institutional care is best for children.

Children are placed in Christian families while the natural family is rehabilitated. During the time the child is cared for the foster family seeks to befriend and support the child's family. When re-unification with the natural family is not possible the child is placed in a permanent family. Social workers also provide support for natural families and foster families.

* *Playgroup*
Offers pre-school children the opportunity of mixing with other children of their own age.

* *Pre-school Music*
Helps to meet some of the social needs of mothers and their children in the community and provides an opportunity for Christian mothers to rub shoulders with others and so develop friendships. A variety of musical experiences are provided for 2-5year olds. This includes finger games, playing instruments and dancing. These help build and develop skills appropriate to this age level in a fun environment. A time slot of 15 minutes is available for parents to mix and mingle at the conclusion of each session.

* *Prison Ministry*
Seeks to enter the prisons and minister to those serving sentences.

* *Refugee/New Settler Habilitation*
To show Christ's love and concern for the poor by assisting in the settlement of refugees into the New Zealand 'way of life' so that they can eventually contribute towards and enrich our multicultural society. A sponsoring group is expected to provide material help and to assist the sponsored family in learning about the community and gaining access to its services eg.–
    * help find accommodation at reasonable rental for the first few weeks
    * provide basic furniture and household essentials
    * find suitable employment
    * assist in English language learning
    * settle children in schools
    * assist the family to make contact with other members of their ethnic group within the local community.

* *Rehabilitation Farm*
This operated for a period of time and was involved in the rehabilitation of young people who wished to get off drugs and alcohol. Also sought to provide a healthy environment in

which to learn new skills with animals and plants. Produced vegetables for the local markets and ran a piggery.

* School Committees, Local Clubs

There are many opportunities for Christians to be involved in local clubs, service organisations and Boards of trustees for schools.

We believe that this offers us excellent openings to be involved in valuable local activities and provides us with the opportunity of making friends with those outside our immediate church network.

* Senior Citizens

Visits on a weekly basis to the rest homes within the area for an hour-long, interesting programme. Mothers take children, as old people love to see children around and this can be a rewarding commitment to mothers at home during the day. On occasions to take some of the elderly folk out for an outing.

* Sponsored Holidays

Provide subsidised or completely free holidays for families within the community which never have an opportunity to have a family holiday.

* Titirangi Care Centre

This functions as a drop in centre at the local community hall each Wednesday. Aims to meet the needs of people who are seeking to have a quality of life beyond just physical survival, by ministering to them in body, mind, emotions and spirit.

Groups operate offering learning opportunities to build self esteem. Speakers are invited to speak on topics of interest. Creche, lunches, a 'care' table and communal singing are all provided. Counselling and support is provided for those in crisis.

* Unemployment Schemes

Run for several years in cooperation with the Government. Provided the opportunity for young people to learn work skills, good habits, handling of money, and better health. Also provided work for needy people within the community.

* *Vegetable Co-op*

Provides families in the community, particularly those under financial stress, with fresh fruit and vegetables at more affordable prices. Gives a regular point of contact with local families, thereby giving further opportunity to demonstrate and encourage Christian living. Members pay a set amount each week for a box which contains varieties of common vegetables and fruit sufficient for a family of two adults and two children. Price is about half of normal retail and operation is completely non-profit. Co-op can be used as a practical outreach ministry by sponsoring boxes for families in need.

* *Wide Variety of Youth Groups*

Caters for children from 11 through to mid twenties. School clubs, youth at risk, Bible studies, activity programmes and numerous other activites are run.

STUDY GUIDE

These studies will best be used in small groups within an atmosphere of prayer and honest sharing. They should not be treated as intellectual abstractions and are geared to help people to face issues which will cause growth in the Christian faith.

Introduction

Personal testimony has a place in evangelism and in church life. Paul recounted his testimony several times see Acts 22, Acts 26, 2 Cor 6:3-10 and 2 Cor 11:21-33.

1. Discuss the strengths and weaknesses of recounting personal testimonies.
2. In groups of 2 or 3 recount turning points or significant people or times in your Christian walk. Pray together and thank God for those who have been an influence for good in your life.
3. Prepare a brief, written testimony of your Christian life, things you would wish to tell a non-Christian who may ask you about this. Share these together the next time you meet.

Chapter 1. Renewal

Many congregations have been impacted in some way by charismatic renewal over the past few years.

1. What are some of the strengths and weaknesses of charismatic renewal?
2. Discuss some of the tensions that you, or others you know of, have experienced in such situations.
3. What steps should leadership take to seek to reduce such tensions in a local congregation?
4. What steps should members of the congregation take to reduce such tensions?

Chapter 2. The Ministry of the Spirit

Select some of the aspects of the ministry of the Holy Spirit in the life of Jesus listed in this chapter. Discuss the practical implications of these in the lives of His followers today.

Find other references in the New Testament to these ministries of the Holy Spirit in the life of the followers of Christ.

Chapter 3. Gifts of the Spirit

1. Knowing what God wants us to do in various situations of life is very important. In what ways does God lead His people today? Discuss ways in which you personally have sensed God leading you.
2. Place yourself on the 'sign gifts' learning curve. If you were previously in a different position on this curve how were you able to make a change? When 'sign gifts' are being discussed, how do you react to others in different positions on this curve? How do those in a different position to you on the curve react to you? What can we learn from this as to how we should react to those who hold different views to us in these matters?
3. How often do you pray with people to be healed? What are some of the things that prevent you doing this?

Chapter 4. Change

You are members of a congregation (organisation) and you feel that there is a change needed in a particular area of of your congregation's life. Use the following outline to plan a strategy to implement this change. (Remember that you are part of a Christian organisation!!!)

i. Clearly identify the area which needs changing.
ii. Prepare a written statement of what you would like the final outcome of this proposed change to be. Also outline the advantages of your proposed change over the current situation.
iii. What role does the leadership of your congregation have in implementing this change? How do you plan to share your proposals with them?
iv. Identify those in your congregation:

*   who would definitely support this change
*   who would definitely not support this change
*   whose position on the proposed change you would not be sure of.

How would you approach people in these three categories? Who is best suited to approach people in these three categories?

v. What resources are available to you to effectively communicate the need for this change? ie tapes, articles, books, resource people.
vi. How will you make sure that Christian grace and loving relationships are maintained within the congregation while you are seeking to implement this change?
vii. What part does prayer and ministry of the Spirit have in producing this change?
viii. If you fail to implement this change, how will you personally handle this matter in a positive way?

Chapter 5. Reaching into the Community

1. Identify some of the people you have contact with – relatives, neighbours, work mates etc.
    What needs do you know of?
    Can you identify these on the Maslow hierarchy?
    Plan and pray about ways in which you could serve these people by ministering to their needs.
2. What degree of credibility does your congregation have with those in the local community?
    How much does the local community know about your congregation's activities?
    Are any of these activities particularly appropriate to them? Do they meet their needs?
3. Get a group of people together to carefully design a survey to investigate the impact your congregation is having on the local community. Include some questions which ask those in the community what they would like your congregation to provide. Use this survey on 100 randomly selected homes around your congregational base to assess the community's awareness of your congregation's activities.

Chapter 6. Words, Deeds and Signs

1. The following is a list of some of the verses in the New Testament which talk about 'good works' or doing good.

      Matt 5:16, Luke 6:27, 2 Cor 9:8,
      Gal 6:10, Eph 2:10, 1 Thess 5;15,
      2 Tim 3:16-17, Heb 10:24,
      1 Pt 2;12, 1 Pt 2:15.

   According to these verses what are some of the resources we have that help us to do good works?

      To whom should good works be done?
      What will be the results?
      Discuss what practical steps you can take to obey what the Spirit of God is saying to us in these portions.

2. Try to estimate how much of your congregation's evangelism is by words, by deeds, by signs. If there is a gross imbalance suggest ways in which this could be addressed. Pray about this matter together.

3. What role do we as human beings play in the area of signs? Is this just God's work? Does He involve human beings in this activity? What do the following verses say about this?

      Matt 9:27-29, 13:57-58, 17:14-21,
      John 14:11-14, Matt 7:7-8, James 4:1-3
      1 Cor 12:9-10.

   What other portions of the New Testament give us insights into this?

4. Some Christians have got involved in social work and have then lost the cutting edge of evangelism. How can we guard against this happening?

Chapter 7. Wanted – Unifying Theme

Get each person in the group to list in order of priority what they feel are the three most important things God wants Christians to do or be.

Tabulate these.

   How many different areas were listed?
   You will probably find a diversity of opinion within the group, why do you think this is so?

Discuss how the theme of the Kingdom of God is an over-arching theme which can integrate these different emphases.

Chapter 8. The Kingdom of God

1. Demonstration and extension of the Kingdom of God were two aspects of Jesus ministry while here on earth. In what ways can we engage in these two activities today?
2. If the Kingdom of God is here but not fully, how should this affect our praying for healing?
3. Read Romans 8:18-39. This portion deals realistically with the Christian life. Notice the references to groaning (v18-26) – discuss what this means to us today.
   It also points out that we are conquerors (v28-39). How can these two aspects of our Christian life be reconciled? Discuss together the dangers of pessimistic Christianity and triumphalistic Christianity.

Chapter 9. Evidence of the Kingdom of God

Share together any evidences of the Kingdom of God that you have read about or observed recently in your own life or in the lives of others around you. How did these affect you? Did those outside of the Kingdom of God observe them? What impact did these have on them?

Chapter 10. Conflict of the Kingdoms

1. Men and women are created in the image of God, to enjoy fellowship with God and with freedom to choose. Discuss how sin has affected these three unique characteristics of human beings. How does salvation affect these areas?
2. From the point of view of the conflict of the kingdoms, discuss the practical implications that the following verses have for us.

   2 Cor 10:3-5, Eph 1:17-23, Eph 6:10-18,
   2 Thess 2:5-12, 2 Tim 2:3-4, Heb 2:14-16,
   1 John 1:5-10, 1 John 4:4.

What do these verses tell us about the Christian's resources in this warfare?

3. Ephesians 2:1-3 indicates that sin comes at us from
    three sources:
    i.   the philosophies and influences of the world around
         us – v1, 'the ways of this world.' (Gal 6:14)
    ii. the devil and his forces – v1, 'the ruler of the
         kingdom of the air.' (Heb 2:14-15)
    iii. our old sinful nature - v3, 'gratifying the cravings
         of our sinful nature and following its desires and
         thoughts.' (Rom 6:6-7)

The verse in brackets after each of the above, indicates that
these three sources of sin have been dealt with by the cross (ie
the death and resurrection) of Christ. Read these verses and
discuss ways in which we can practically experience the
victory which God means us to enjoy over these three sources
of sin.

Chapter 11. Money, Materialism and the Kingdom of God

WARNING!! This is a controversial topic. People will
hold widely differing points of view. Emotions may run high
during this discussion. Answers to the problems are not
simple.

ENCOURAGEMENT!! Great rewards await those who
will confront this topic with faith, courage, honesty and
obedience.

1. Discuss ways in which the E Stanley Jones quote at the
    beginning and end of this chapter could be
    implemented in your congregation.
2. Analyse a few TV advertisements. Do they appeal to –
        status,
        selfish ambition,
        security,
    How many appeal to greed?
    Are the claims they make wholly true, partly true,
    untrue?
    How should we train children when it comes to
    observing TV ads?
3. Discuss ways in which you could live more simply.
4. Break the cycle. Select a Christian project which is
    needing money. Pray about choosing an object of
    value (not an 'essential' household item), sell it and

give the money towards this project. If a group should do this a considerable amount of money could be raised.
5. Are you in debt? Seek budgeting advice.
6. Discuss with a close friend the hold money and material possessions have on you. Pray together and seek to be accountable to each other in some of the areas you struggle with.
7. There are many topics raised in this chapter. Select some others and discuss the implications of these in your lives.

Chapter 12. The Church and the Kingdom of God
1. Discuss ways in which you can measure the goals of your congregation in terms of the Kingdom of God.
2. Estimate how many hours you personally spend in church activities each week. How can other areas of your life be more productive for the Kingdom of God? Prayerfully discuss with other people in your group your occupation. Seek the guidance of the Holy Spirit as to how to bring greater effectiveness for the Kingdom of God to this area of your life . Remember a job is not just to make money, it's an opportunity to 'seek first he Kingdom of God.'
3. The text suggests that three main roles for the congregation are worship, fellowship and equipping. Which do you feel is weakest in your congregation? Make some positive suggestions as to how this could be improved.
4. At the end of the section headed, 'What role for the congregation?' six points are made. Discuss these with reference to yourself and your own congregation.
5. Discuss the Snyder quote at the end of the chapter.

Chapter 13. Putting it all Together
1. There are nine points listed in the text which are suggested as features of a modified model for the congregation. Discuss these in relation to your own congregation. Make positive suggestions and consider the possibility of sharing them with your congregation's

leadership.
2. List the people in your congregation who are already actively involved in community and para-church ministries.

    Do these people know of each other's involvement? Does networking occur between the various groups?
    Are they encouraged publicly?
    Does the congregation pray for them?
    In what ways can you support them?
3. What community ministries do people from other local churches operate?
4. Are there any ways in which combined congregational community ministries can operate?
5. Discuss together your personal involvement in community ministry. Where do you stand regarding the priorities of biological, church and world family?
6. List the personal gifts, skills and resources which you have that could possibly be used to minister to people in the community. If you feel God is wanting you to commence a community ministry pray about this with others. Work through the questions under the section 'How to start ministries to the community' and discuss it with your church leadership.

Appendix I Kingdom Manifesto

a. Read the Manifesto through aloud in the group in one sitting.
b. Read and study it personally in an attitude of prayer, worship and expectation.
c. Read through the suggested biblical references for each section. Are they relevant to the issues? Suggest others, including biblical stories, parables etc.
d. Pray with new meaning and dedication our Lord's prayer, 'Your Kingdom come, your will be done on earth as it is in heaven.'
e. Allow the Lord's words in Matt 6:33 – 'Seek first the Kingdom of God and His righteousness' – to impact all the areas of your life.
f. Suggest to your church leadership that this be used as

a basis of study for house groups, etc. Recommend that teaching is given in your congregation on this important topic.

Preamble

1. In our modern 20th century society how does Jesus challenge to 'Seek first the Kingdom of God' give us a focus for living?
2. Why has the theme of the 'Kingdom of God,' so central to Jesus ministry, been neglected by present-day Christians?

We Confess . . .

As you read this confession ask the following questions.

1. Do we put our aims and interests above those of others – our Lord, our family, our church, our neighbours?
2. Do we keep our spiritual life separate from other areas of our life?
3. Do we speak up in situations of injustice or corrupt practice or do we try to ignore such?
4. Do we find it hard to work harmoniously with others in church life or in our occupation?
5. Add your own confessions.

Biblical Base

1. At what times in the history of Israel do we see God's Kingdom rule most effectively demonstrated?
2. Jesus inaugurated a new dimension of the Kingdom of God when He came to earth. He healed people, fed people, performed miracles, drove out evil spirits. Why then did the religious leaders so violently reject Him? Why do people reject Him today?
3. When Jesus said the Kingdom is 'near' (Mark 1:15) did He mean that it was a geographical region, an institution to join or a new reign which would lead to a new set of relationships? Discuss what this means to us today.

The King and His Kingdom

1. In Luke 4:16-22 Jesus claimed that He was fulfilling the prophecies of Isaiah 61:1-2. Should these prophecies

    be taken literally? Compare the answer that Jesus gave to the questions of John the Baptist in Matthew 11:4-6.

2. Is the great commission that Jesus gave to His disciples (Matt 28:18-20), a continuation of His emphasis on the Kingdom of God or is it a new commandment? The first part of v20 may give us a key here. What did Jesus teach?

3. The term 'king' and 'kingdom' are used regularly in the first three Gospels. With the variety of political situations on earth today, many people today have no practical understanding of what these terms mean. What other terms could be used to explain these concepts?

Signs of the Kingdom

1. A sign is a visible evidence of a special relationship (eg a wedding ring), whereas a signpost shows the difference between the right path and the wrong path. How does the Church fulfil both these roles?

2. Discuss examples of people you know who have come into the new birth. How has this been a sign of the Kingdom to those around them?

3. Are you aware of people who have suffered for righteousness sake? How effective a sign has this been of the Kingdom of God? Have they also been a signpost?

4. There are seven signs listed in the Kingdom Manifesto. What other signs of the Kingdom of God are there?

Entering the Kingdom

1. The first three Gospels focus on Jesus teaching on the Kingdom of God while John gives more attention to the new birth and eternal life. Is eternal life synonymous with the Kingdom and being born again with entering the Kingdom? (See John 3).

2. If the Kingdom is open to all races and classes of people, then why did Jesus show greater concern for the poor, the hungry, the sick, the disabled, the widow and the prostitute? Have we failed to minister to the poor and weaker sections of our society or are there other reasons why they have rejected the gospel?

The Kingdom of God and the Church

1. Some people believe that the Church is the Kingdom. Others say that the Church is what is important now while the Kingdom of God is in the future. Is there a third way of viewing the Church and the Kingdom of God?
2. How can the Church be an agent for peace and reconciliation if it is divided within itself?
3. How can we demonstrate unity while respecting diversity of worship and witness to the world?
4. Someone once said, 'The Church is the only society that exits for the sake of those who are not its members.' Do you think this is true? Discuss this statement.

Opposition to the Kingdom of God

1. If Jesus disarmed all evil powers and authorities triumphing over them by the cross (Col 2:15), why is there so much suffering in the world today? Is it because the Church has has failed to be like salt – restraining evil, and has been unfaithful about being light – proclaiming the whole gospel?
2. If we believe we are dead with Christ and risen with Him how then can we overcome:
   > sexual temptation
   > the love of money and material possessions
   > family disputes
   > a domineering spirit
   > resentment towards those who have hurt us?

The Kingdom and Human Relationships

1. If life in the Kingdom of God means 'To act justly, to love mercy and to walk humbly with your God,' (Micah 6:8) what practical steps can Christians take to be peacemakers and lovers of justice in labour disputes, riots and acts of terrorism and in religious and racial conflicts? Think carefully about the implications of justice, mercy and humility.
2. In order to stand for the Kingdom values of peace, justice and mercy, should Christians participate in protest marches, wear badges and slogan T shirts, risk

      police arrest, write letters to the newspapers? How do we relate our call to peace and justice with our call to evangelism and church planting?

3. In what ways will the practice of a simpler lifestyle make us better stewards of money and material possessions?

The Kingdom and Society

1. Social concern has been described as:

        a partner to evangelism
        a bridge for evangelism
        a consequence of evangelism.

Discuss the truth of these three statements.

How could your congregation be more involved in social concern?

2. Some Christians think that the sermon on the Mount is not for this age but for the future. Others feel it is an impossible ethical standard. What do you think about this? What current aspects of your life need to be rejected if you are to live according to this teaching of Jesus?

3. Ecological considerations have become a major focus around the world. Green is in!! Christians should be concerned about these issues because we are stewards of God's creation. What practical things can we be engaged with in this area?

4. In our dialogue with people of other faiths and cultures, how can we respect their beliefs and values and yet witness to our belief that only Christ can transform them and their values?

The Kingdom of God and the Future

1. In the light of the return of Christ and the full establishment of His Kingdom, how should we currently be living?

2. Discuss some of the tensions we currently experience between the 'already' and 'not yet fully' of the Kingdom of God.

Commitment to the Kingdom of God

Christ is calling us to costly discipleship and servanthood and to be faithful stewards of all we have and are. How should this affect our:

i. Time.

Think of priorities, planning, areas where we waste time. Is it sometimes harder to say 'no' than 'yes'? See the parable of the banquet (Luke 14:15-24).

ii. Money and possessions.

Where is your treasure? (Matt 6:21) Do you budget? What percentage of income is spent on recreation? How are we affected by advertising? Do we constantly hunger for more 'things'? How much do you give to God? Compare the parables of the rich fool (Luke 12:13-21) and the hidden treasure/pearl (Matt 13:44-45).

iii. Abilities and skills.

Do we own these or are we stewards of them? How well have you developed yours? Compare the parable of the talents (Lk 19:22-27) and the tenants (Matt 21:33-44). Ask God for opportunities and courage to use these abilities and skills creatively and effectively within the Kingdom of God.

Final Summation

Reflect on some of the things you have learned during this study. What decisions have you made? What decisions do you still need to make? Remember that being hearers only and not doers means we are deceiving ourselves.(James 1:22-25) Read further books which develop the theme of the Kingdom of God. Seek out those who are of like mind and pray, study and stand together about issues which you feel are important. Constantly challenge your own vision (and that of others) of the Kingdom of God. Count the cost and start to build on Kingdom values.